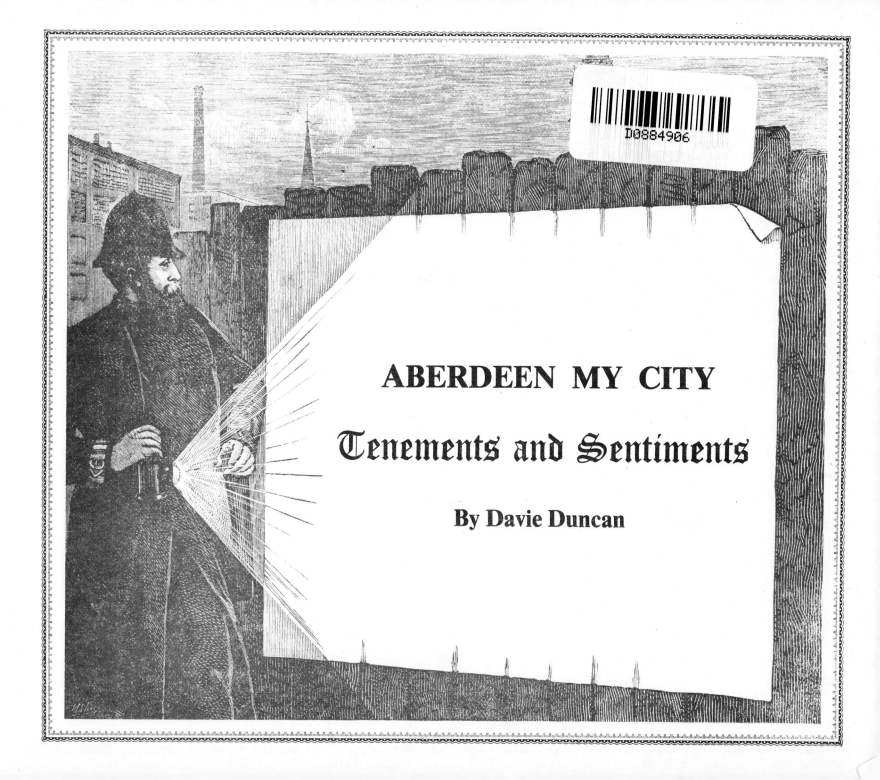

ABERDEEN MY CITY

Tenements and Sentiments

By Davie Duncan

UNION COURT

FINDLAYS COURT

McKAY'S COURT or CAN'LE CLOSE

PORTHILL CLOSE

PATERSON'S COURT

Gallowgate looking towards Farquhar Place ropeworks. "The win' may blaw thin'', but "the granite chips'', those true Aberdonians, will aye survive. The buildings faced Mount Hooly and Nelson Street, and the wind does play freely over their site — the roundabout, which is of Hyde Park Corner proportions.

Bars, Barracks and Boorachies.
The Gallowgate looking south: (foreground properties cleared c1963). No. 173, with its gable end to the street, was probably the oldest in the area; forestairs gave access to the upper floor. Diagonally opposite is the Berry Street opening, where Guiseppe Nardi had his celebrated fish and chip shop. Bernard Balfour describes his family home at No. 1 Berry Street, (birthplace of two teachers, an M.P. and Manager of The Blind Asylum): "It was reputed to have been a residence of a Georgian doctor c1790, but since partitioned and sub-divided. There was a lavatory in the basement to serve dozens of people in the house, and was of early Victorian design; an iron stirrup handle was pulled up, which opened a sluice along a pipe below the long wooden board with a hole in the middle. Gas lighting had been introduced in the twentieth century, and the lead pipes simply ran along the wall at head-height. If a leak was suspected, a lit candle was taken along the pipe until the gas ignited . . . then wet soap was placed over the hole; left to dry, and life went on as normal''.

"The Causeyman''. Gallowgate Courts, (southern side), at the turn of this century.

For Mum and Dad :—
"The open flooerie aye depends on the reets it springs fae".

THE NEW PORTHILL SCHOOL
—FROM THE NORTH—

GEORGE LEIPER DUNCAN'S PLEA FOR JUSTICE:—
("Tommy Atkins, [Foot Soldier], aye carried the load", however).

To the Minister of Pensions Complaint and Persocitii

Statement of Appeal

Sir, On Oct. 27th 1926 I was taken suddenly ill and for two weeks I was confined to bed and was attended by my panel doctor and he said I was suffering from my war disability and I have been incapacitated from work since that time. Ever since I was gassed I have always had these symptoms on me and a giddyness in the head as though I was going to fall down. Since I was gassed I have been confined to bed at different periods of time and this has prevented me from working. Now what I would like to get at is this Why the Ministry of Pensions is so determined not to let me get my treatment allowances when I am badly with my war disability. There is something queer about this altogether and I would like if you would give proper attention to this statement and therefore give me the justice I am entitled to.

7-1-27

Geo Leiper Duncan

I was born into 1915 Aberdeen, with all its heritage from the past; this was, in my case, a dilapidated house at 113 Skene Street, inconspicuous amongst the menial parade of tenements and dingy shops that divided Chapel Street from Summer Street. This was the drab environment that cradled my first maturing years and imprinted its experience in my young impressionable mind; filling my eyes with pain and pleasure.

Loyalties were moulded and tempered in this background of human frailty, honed by their subterfuge for the needs to survive. The wordly scab of indifference that divided our neighbours and the decaying primitive dwellings we had as shelters for our families created paradoxically a way of sympathy, compassion and help that suffused a little piece of Heaven. This gave us a ray of hope, hinting that there must be a way out of our squalor; evading the dead hand of poverty.

These feelings came more conscious and apparent when my Mum left Skene Street to stay at 2 Minister Lane, a small, narrow street to which there was public access via a close from Skene Street. This byeway I was to get to know too well. Here, amongst the various families with whom I became familiar and a part of, was the stage upon which Mum, my brother Edward, sister Jeannie, Georgina and myself grew up together as a family.

Mum, as I realised later on, lived apart from Dad; this one thing made a significant difference in my lifestyle, for its influence has changed and modulated my personality to face up to the many problems and decisions that I had to shoulder personally.

My first real experience of individuality is associated in my mind with 2 Minister Lane. Our front door was one of four leading off a dark dingy lobby, which in turn was approached by an outside stair. There were no lights in the lobby, but our rooms faced onto Kidd Street and Minister Lane corner where there was a street lamp which just happened to be fixed to the wall only a few feet from our living room window; the antiquated lamp had a huge inverted bowl, with the gas mantle shining within. When I looked outside upon dark winter nights, the light from the lighted gas mantle created pools of light upon the pavement below, which contrasted with the flickering light of gas in our room with its coal fire and heating oven, painted black besides the steel components and ash pan catching the embers as they filtered down from the burning coals, or whatever you had to burn for cheapness and heat.

Mum and me at 2 Minister Lane.

The Aberdeen

One large single-head Davis Efficiency Boiling-Burner; single revolving Grill Burner with fixed Deflector Plates; all burners fitted with gas and air adjusters. Gas connexion either side.

Price with Pan and Grid
29/6

There was a gas ring on the range; a gas tube connecting it, with a rubber holder to the gas pipe. This was always wearing to a state beyond repair, with the usual leakage of gas. Perhaps, the use of the gas pipe to set alight the stubborn fuel in the fireplace may have been the reason for the necessary renewals of gas tubes and rubber connections.

I remember the brass double bed in the corner, beside the window; the mahogany ogee chest of drawers, the wooden shelf (fixed on the wall at the door side) laden with pots, pans and kettle plus various other objects; the ochred walls and dado of varnished wallpaper. The lino on the floor was patched and worn. A small bedroom led off the living room and was lit by skylight windows. One bed occupied a corner of this room. The outstanding feature of our living room was the steel fender enclosing the pipe-clayed stone front of the fireplace, other parts of which had been painted with black lead. The steel fender etc. were made shining bright with emery paper and "elbow grease". The task of maintaining this homely feature gave me a sense of stability; security could only be a day to day experience.

I remember lying in Mum's bed; a man looking down at me, opening my mouth with an ivory stick, probing my throat; after a little time he turned to Mum and spoke inaudibly to her. After he had gone, Mum took me up in her arms to fondle and comfort me with great affection; her love for me had locked away the secret that I had infantile paralysis in my right leg until I tried to walk naturally.

Loving, kindly Mum was the anchor that we all clung to; for her courage kept us together as a family. She did the most menial and hardest tasks for a pittance, without complaining, doing everything humanly possible to ensure that I could walk. I remember distinctly taking the first faltering footsteps within four chairs; getting balance and confidence; after a few experiments of this nature, I was able to walk upright like any other child.

On the first occasion of triumphing over this disability, I was bosied by a Mum's loving arms, and the tears that ran down her furrowed cheeks were ample evidence of her pleasure, now that I would be able to walk and play normally with the children in Minister Lane. In fact, I had found my feet in the family.

Being able to walk, widened my experience with people and places. I met other children; mixing with them as a playmate, selecting pals and sorting out of egos — very necessary for survival. Brutality still dwelt amongst us; I, at this young age understood that pain and neglect; perceived the walking evidence of it that stalked us all. Our family, so fortunate of families to be so certain of our Mum's tender heart and loving care. The welfare and spiritual needs of the family no saint could have bettered when it came to the courage required to summon the will to earn a living from hard taskmasters. This was the basic "founds" that guided me in my lifetime, and gave a sense of moral balance and understanding to bring social justice. One great lesson that I learned from it all was that principles demanded sacrifices, and if your principles are leavened with the Christian spirit, what can persuade you to abandon them?

As I grew older, and being in the company of my pals, I began to "extend my scenes". I found out about the uses of the "backies", outside W.C.'s and rows of delapidated cellars that had more rubbish in them than quantities of coal. The wash house with its two deep sinks and boiler fire providing hot water; the pipe leading away from it to emerge through the roof, spewing out black clouds of soot all over the place. In the corner stood the mammoth, a heavy cast iron mangle which was operated by two wooden rollers, through which the sheets and clothes were "ca'ed" with the help of a large handle and wheel; the rollers could be adjusted to take any thickness of sheets, blankets or clothes. Every tenant had a time allotted officially for their washing day during the week — what an upheaval in the house . . . the early rise in the morning; filling the "biler" with water to be heated by a fire that was kindled by sleepy young hands. "The stirring stick", which was long and worn, pressed the dirt out of the washing. The ropes had to be stretched from pole to pole; the clothes poles, in readiness to hoist the rope laden with washing, enabled bedclothes to get a good airing if the elements were favourable.

The washing day sometimes meant that the blankets or sheets weren't exactly dry. We had to make do with anything we had handy as makeshift covering: coats and old threadbare curtains had a new lease of life, to keep the family warm. Five or six to a bed was a common feature in our homes; or in a lot of cases a "shakky doon" on the floor — the staple comfort for warmth being a stoneware hot water bottle, or on many an occasion, hot bricks wrapped in "cloots" were the bedwarmers.

Tenements, by and large were overcrowded, with primitive facilities, (or lack of them); there being no sink in the lobby; just a water tap placed outside the back door. This was the only source of water supplying the tenants' needs in all kinds of weather, the whole year round. No wonder filth penetrated everywhere . . . helped by damp walls and ceilings that bred bugs by the score. Many families bore the little pink bites of their tormentors. With the lack of running water at hand, hygiene wasn't enough to do away with them. Every night and morning, bean comb exercises to eradicate the lice, and application of paraffin was the only known antidote; the smell was always in your nostrils, being a constant reminder of your place in society. I certainly learned fast that the children who came from the better type of neighbour-hoods, and could afford pennies at the nearby sma' shoppies on sweeties, were a race apart. I wondered why; and sometimes I felt pity for these other children. Some of these children, without apparent reason, shared their pieces or sweets with some of us. When I look back, these bairns may have been touched by compassion; felt a sense, not of guilt of having, but a guilt of non-sharing.

Household Hints

DRYNESS

Old newspapers spread under the counterpane, or laid smoothly, inside dresses folded for packing, prevent creases. When storing a carpet, roll in paper soaked with ammonia or turpentine, and then in newspaper. Old felt hats may be profitably utilised for making comfortable soles for shoes and slippers. Cut a piece of stout paper the size and shape of sole required, lay it along the side of a bowler hat, outline with chalk, and then cut carefully with a sharp knife or scissors. An old cycle tyre's outer cover will make as good rubber heels as you can buy. Cupboards can be kept dry by placing a small box filled with lime upon a shelf. Beds can be checked for dampness by placing a looking glass between the sheets for a few minutes. If on removal the glass is clouded the sheets are not sufficiently dried and had better be removed.

Inside the house, the family had to fend for themselves; except Dad, who visited us infrequently. We young ones had to hold and fold the clothes when Mum was doing the ironing. She used either the "flat iron", with its solid base, which she heated over the fire or gas-ring. Alternatively the other heating iron had a compartment which held a specially shaped brick. This brick could be made very hot then popped into the compartment and used accordingly.

The interiors of the tenements in Minister Lane left a lot to be desired: the staircases, especially the treads of the steps, were virtually worn away; the big knots of wood sticking up from the well-trodden floors of the lobbies and landings. The scruffy, pitted, broken, ochred plaster walls made the darkness and dreariness more depressing. The view from the murky landing window onto Minister Lane seemed like an unsurmountable granite wall of depression; alleviated only by a glimpse of a nice residence with an open-fronted cobbled yard, owned by people named Mitchell; their son I occasionally saw, but never played with. The other side of the lane was occupied by the timber merchant and sawyer; his planks of wood built up to season. We often climbed and jumped on top of the planks, and for sure, many a private feud was settled there, with the bare knuckles; (the good eens didn't win all the time). The rest of the Lane was back door access for some of the tenements in Kidd Street. Kidd Street used to be a narrow street, running from Summer Street to Chapel Street. At the top end, on the right hand side from Summer Street, a huddled mass of tenements stretched the whole length of the street, with another timber yard and building standing apart from this rookery; one or two tenanted houses standing alongside. Kidd Street was named after Dr. Kidd the minister, whose sermons were published during the time of his ministry at Gilcomston Parish Church. His name was also given to Minister Lane. Anything in common the local folk had had with Dr. Kidd or his religion in my time was never apparent. The families that I knew were the salt of the earth: the Browns, Websters, Simpsons, and Smalls; all of Minister Lane. Theirs was an enriched poverty that felt compassion for their neighbours in want or distress. They gave out of their little, that it hurt. They may not have had the bible in their hands, but they had the fullness of heart that the Lord Jesus preached and practised about his meaning of giving.

These were the days when evictions were a common sight: the landlords increasingly demanding their pound of flesh. They had no feelings of what they did. Often, the help of the police was used to force these hopeless, downtrodden families into the street, whatever the weather; their only alternative choice was "Old Mill", the Poor's House; and once there, inside those walls, they became a family divided, perhaps never to know or meet one another again. Despite this horrendous side of our fate, we children scratched some pleasure from life when we met in "wir backies", playing at "horsies", or "tick & tack"; climbing onto the cellar roofs, playing at "beddies" there. Everything bad was forgotten in the magic hour of play. Even at this early stage in life, it became common knowledge to me about "the suicide" that had cut their throat or put their head in the oven with the gas turned on, using their last few pence. These were the casualties of hopelessness or grinding poverty; or maybe both. Sometimes we saw small white coffins, carried by men wearing black clothes; we thought they were the "bogey men" — they scared us stiff.

It was the lot of the children in this neighbourhood to wear parish clothing and second hand "hand-me-downs". The meals, meanest of fare, contributed to their way of life. Even at this level, far too many families struggled in more unmentionable conditions. We, who survived, owe a great debt to our parents; who, with their limitations pledged their present and future with the pawnbroker and small corner shop that gave them "Tick" in order to eke out and make their customer's poverty more tolerable. The trust of these shopkeepers was amazingly, and largely never, abused. In fact, for many households throughout the years, this was their only lifeline of survival.

Honesty and integrity were seldom betrayed; only death changed the faces. Even in death, many good people suffered the last rebuff from life: a pauper's funeral.

Edward, Georgina and Jeannie being older than me, were attending Skene Street School. I was the only one with my mother so had to tag along with her. Sometimes Mum, three or four other women used to organise a seance which took place once or twice a week at different homes. This required us to visit, so I was taken along to the seance. I distinctly remember the moment when they put out the gaslights and sat around the table, with hands laid out flat on the table top. I was sitting about two yards away, when one of the women began to speak in an unfamiliar voice. She spoke for

a little while in the silent room then I noticed that the table began to rock; then it rose about six inches. For a long second there was no sound before screaming began, chairs falling over and a mad rush to the door so that the light of day could be let in. It was quite some time before sanity was restored and things sorted out. I still maintain that something did happen in that room which wasn't natural. I did have contact with other seance gatherings, but a single experience that I had personally at the age of four which occurred at home when Mum was unwell, still feels uncanny to me. I remember the experience very vividly; Mum was lying in her brass bed, still feeling weak, when she asked me to get something for her out of the top drawer of the ogee chest. I was just opening the drawer, when I happened to glance around and saw an old tubby man, who wore his cloth cap "aft taeglie", sitting on the bedside chair, holding a walking stick in his hand. His hands were covered with khaki mittens, but the remarkable thing was that he was displaying his forefinger, which had been sliced off at the joint; the cut actually showing blood-red. When I moved to approach him, he smiled, then vanished. I turned around to my Mum and told her what I had just seen, but she "pooh-pooed" it and mildly suggested that I had been dreaming, but I persisted that this manifestation was of a genuine nature. Eventually Mum admitted to me that it was my late grandfather whom I had seen; he had died a few years earlier. The interest of the seance, and the tangible implications of the occult as applied to their everyday lives were firmly entrenched as some sort of faith by the women around this neighbourhood; not surprisingly, when they bore the brunt of the dank, dingy, gritty confined living standards that go hand in hand with unemployment and poverty. "Those who dwelt in darkness" did see "a great light".

When you are four years old, you have more latitude to wander about. This meant for me, going out from Minister Lane up to Chapel Street and discovering that there was a public urinal there. I came to use it time and time again; it fascinated me. I felt that bit taller or older every time I used it. In a way I was meeting adults strangers, and beginning to shed my childhood innocence for a mature approach to people and their surroundings. The Chapel Street that I knew at this age, stretched down hill from Huntly Street to Skene Street. I had often seen a house that sat well back from the street frontage, with its long garden. I wondered who might stay in this "castle" of my dreams; proceeding down the left hand side from Huntly Street there was a plumber's shop and then the aforementioned urinal. Granite does not age graciously, particularly when exterior walls require repointing. My impressions of the congested mass of tenements grew dingier by degrees until at last I reached a dark and dreary closie that yawned before me like "The Black Hole of Calcutta". Crossing the street at this point, I discovered a newsagent's shop, which I subsequently went into when my funds were solvent and bought a sweetie smoking pipe that was coloured pink. Passing by even worse habitations I came upon a home cooking shop which sold pies and other tempting delicacies. Somehow I never made it moneywise so that I could sample the wares that they had on offer.

At this age, by and large, one remembers only the trivial things, but seeing a bi-plane for the first time, seems in my imagination to have permanently risen above the plateau of trivia. This event happened during a warm day, with brilliant sunshine and I was alone in the "backie", standing outside the W.C., when I heard a thunderous noise coming down from the sky, and saw the bi-plane flying in the heavens, accomplishing amazing feats of twisting, turning, or falling like a leaf towards the earth; then with a scream, soaring back into the sky and doing it all over again. It was just magic; then the war-plane suddenly vanished as it had appeared.

The children in the lane at Kidd Street had an unusual treat occasionally when a man with an organ on a pole entertained them. He was accompanied by a monkey who wore a miniature fez on its head. A small collar around the monkey's neck enabled the long chain to be attached to the organ grinder who played several tunes which meant nothing really to me. The real thrill was the monkey jumping to the ground with a bag in its hand to collect any coppers which might be given. I am afraid to say that his rewards didn't total very much. Itinerant musicians didn't get many pickings in a hard up street like ours, and it was rather noticeable that his appearances grew fewer and fewer. After all, the monkey had to eat. He was replaced by another individual, an Italian with a barrel organ that churned out a different set of tunes. Before he commenced playing, he had about a dozen of us all lined up at the kerbside; then we had to sit down on the pavement itself and listen to his music. What took my attention was a fairly large painting fixed to the side of his instrument. It depicted a front-line trench with British soldiers facing German soldiers in the snow. He must have found us more generous, because he came twice a week.

There was the much looked forward to visit to "The Trainie Parkie", where I played on real grass, and watched the mighty iron monsters huffing and puffing with their steam belching out all over the place. Then came the mad rush to the iron fence for a better view whilst the trains hissed and whistled as they got nearer the Schoolhill railway station. I sniffed the steam and smoke under the spell, unaware that it wasn't good for me.

Another great occasion was going to Union Street to see a procession on parade; the hustle and bustle, the flags flying; marching men and trotting horses. The showpiece was a small 1st World War tank, rumbling its way up imperial Union Street, with a man in uniform perched upon the top as if he were a great hero. The plaudits of the teeming crowds made it a moment to remember. When I was a year or two older, I spent many happy hours playing make believe adventures around the tank which was ideally situated on top of the Broadhill.

My first experience of going beyond my little world, was a trip, by tramcar, from Bridge Street to Torry. To me, this form of conveyance was a different kind of monster, with an open staircase. A long pole was attached to the top deck seemingly by a wire. When we moved on, I heard the clang of a bell dirling in my ears. The sensation of hurtling down Bridge Street and careering around the corner into Guild Street, then bumping up the length of South Market Street towards that narrow bridge leading "o'er the Watter" to God knows where.

I furthered this experience by another tram journey in the opposite direction to Woodside, setting off from "The Queen" on St. Nicholas Street corner. It seemed a never-ending journey, being bumped and jostled by other passengers seated on the long open seats, when they wished to alight, and by the peculiar motions and sudden stops of the tram itself.

Mum had relations who bade at the corner of Western Road, near The Fountain in all its former glory. This was where the tram stopped to let us off. We entered the fruiterers and sweetie shoppie by the "tradesman's entrance"; a green gate, and climbed the stairs to the front door where the names Munro and Ross were displayed on a brass plate. One of the ladies opened the door in haste, and I caught a glimpse of jam making in progress; a big white linen bag crammed with red currants, the juice flowing from it. I was promptly sent down to the "backie" to play on my own, and looking around, I saw that their palings were red-rotten and seething with "horny golachs". Much later we left, never to see them again, but what I remember especially is that they didn't even hand over an apple or a sweetie. I heard subsequently that they were a tight-fisted couple. As we went to catch the tram for home, I heard the loud whistle of a train with steam billowing behind it, rushing into unknown places even further into the country.

It was almost a daily ritual for the boys and girls of the same age as myself to play at "shoppies" or "nurses" in the seclusion of the "backies". The quinies were the nurses, equipped with a towel or big handkerchief over their heads, there imitating real nurses. The loons were the "casualties" who were given First Aid for their wounds and broken bones.

My special nurse was Nan Small, a nice, pretty girl who made a wonderful make believe nurse. My "wounds" or "fractures" always healed well, until one day when Nan herself became a real victim of pneumonia. After a few days of illness she passed away. At the time, when I heard the news of her death, I thought that my world stood still. I just felt full of grief with the certain knowledge that my personal future could not include Nan to attend and care for me when I was hurt. I suppose that this was the inlying reason for my misery, yet if a child's feeling for personal loss could be expressed adequately in words, I knew that something I had liked in a large way had been snatched from me, and I was much the poorer for it.

Around this time, three or four of us (all aged five), would play together. I suppose we did some silly things and maybe irked one or two of the older lads who were not above bullying "the small fry". I remember one afternoon in Kidd Street, where we were playing in peace, when "a boorachie" of such loons came along and roughed us up. After having their fun, they made off to the urinal in Chapel Street. I followed them stealthily, and whilst they were inside for two or three minutes, I swicked in and saw that the seats were occupied. One of them had left a waistcoat on the floor and I promptly went and thrust it down one of the pots, then took the quickest way home. When I reached Minister Lane, it occurred to me that I might have been too hasty; what about the waistcoat? Did he get it or not? Within minutes I heard some shouting at the window. When I dropped the top sash and poked my head out to see who was there, I saw four or five older lads making fierce noises at me, accompanied by threats of punishment at a later date. Making a gesture of defiance I withdrew into the room and slammed up the window, thereby deciding to stay in the house until the "stramash" blew over.

I was coming up to the age of five when that mystery word "school" first started to pop up, with the rest of the family nodding consent to Mum. One very important event preceded my admission to Skene Street School, and that was the appointment that Mum made at the photographer's studio in Schoolhill so that our portrait could be taken as a family. Mum, Edward, Jeannie and myself smartly turned out for the occasion. I often wonder what it cost Mum in terms of hard work and saving to provide us with "swank" clothes for this treat. Whenever I pass up or down Schoolhill, my eyes always wander towards that close and up the ramp to where the studio premises used to be. I look at the peeling door, and time seems to lift its veil, and I am with Mum and the family again, sharing a mutual experience of love that has withstood all the batterings of Fate. The sweetness of that moment still lingers in my nostrils, and when it has passed by, my eyes fill with an involuntary tear. In this regard I am a fortunate man, and thank the good Lord that I have an heirloom that makes me rich indeed.

Games

Place a board on top of a chimney where a fire is lit and smoke the fowk oot. Tie their ootside door handles together loosely. Anither game o' risk is "crack the wheepie". "Humphie Dig" wis a game which prevented your hopping opponent from crossing the street.

The happiest times in my growing life were the cameraderie with other families. We shared events with each other such as Easter picnics and all the excitement of egg rolling; the summer holidays, with all their attendant pleasures, and freedoms, included the Timmer Market, (peas, pluffers and feathery dusters). All these experiences rate alongside two great events of Childhood, Christmas and New Year. Christmas was always magic to me; not that it was Jesus Christ's anniversary; but to my mind, it was a special time within our growing lives and humble homes. The actual nearness of all the bad things that occurred to people like us seemed to recede. This was the one and sure time when we were individuals; our names displayed on the little Christmas cards which Santa Claus, who had driven his reindeer all the way from the North Pole in order to come down our ''lums'' and leave us gifts to make ours a merry Christmas. Tangerines, chocolates and ''clooty'' dumplings were extras that we all looked for.

I never saw a Christmas cracker or a paper hat, but sometimes we got extra pennies. If fate was kind and generous, it could be a silver sixpence. Andrew Carnegie hadn't a look in, and when I look back, was this not the spirit of Christ, the giving and receiving with joy. Perhaps most of us have left behind this special magic that only Jesus Christ gives with our childhood.

I believe in a fashion that Mammon, with his evil tools of the trade, ''envy'', ''greed'' and ''commerce'' has given us many false images that our lives and societies have suffered great damage by our hypocrisy or worship of him.

Hogmanay and the New Year festivities was our time for a visit to the cinema, where every child received an apple or orange. Our parents would buy a favourite comic for us, e.g. ''Comic Cuts'', ''Chips'', ''Rainbow'' or ''The Funny Wonder'', along with everybody's favourite cowboy, ''Charlie''. If our names were on the poor peoples' list, we would get a free picture show, a bag of biscuits or chocolates. That comprised our simple New Year celebrations, yet it reminds me of the poetic wisdom of the words ''Let not Grandeur with disdain smile upon the simple annals of the poor''. Nevertheless, we thought that we were feted like kings.

Nonsense Rhyme

''A peacock pykit a peck o' paper
Oot o' a paper pyock . . .
Pyke, paper, peacock.''

Household Hints

The Fireside

To light: Potato peelings dried in the oven may be used for lighting fires, and make a fire burn up very quickly. Newspapers used to clean cookers should be used immediately while they are hot.

To revive: Dried orange peel placed amongst coals; useful for sick room as there is no noise and resultant pleasant perfume. Place a cork under the hot cinders, and put a match to it.

To save coals: Dissolve a large handful of common wax to a gallon of warm water. Throw this over about 1 cwt. to dry before using. This will make the coal last twice as long.

The winter months were always a time when we had to battle to survive the snow, frost, or rain with very little clothing to wear. It was also another struggle to obtain the fuel with which to provide a source of warmth in our homes. Many differing shapes and sizes of materials were broken up to fit into the fireplace; there was a distinct art in eking it out. The last resource was breaking up a wooden chair just to get warmth. ''Early to bed'' was the economical watchword in most households; many a hot iron stone was wrapped up in a piece of cloot, to be the only heat generated in a double bed, where five or six children slept together. Additional covering was added with the family overcoats. The lights went out early, whether it be gas or paraffin lamp. Coppers were always in short supply for one or the other. In these dingy squalid rooms that we called ''home'', there was the occasional outbreak of ringworm, and I was victim of it. I remember very clearly going upstairs to a Mrs Beverley with Mum, and having a bandage put round my neck. We weren't in long when she gave us a cup of tea and a jammy piece for me along with my ''fly cup''. There was a big ginger cat walking around on the look out for a titbit, (so far without success). When it saw me sitting comfortably on a chair eating my piece, it thought that it had an easy mark, and put out its paw to take its share, but I thought different; and proceeded to push it out of the way, when it flashed out its paw, clooking the skin under my eye, thereby making the blood stream down my cheek. The cup of tea was very hot, and it splashed down over my knees leaving blisters. If it had clawed me a quarter of an inch further up, I would have been one-eyed. Nevertheless, the mark of its scar is still with me. Viewing the incident as a child I considered that apart from this mishap, I had been relatively non-accident prone so far. As a result, I was pampered and petted for the next few days, and I'm glad to say that I still like cats.

As the winter months carried on with their snowy days that left in their wake blocked streets and pavements, neighbours' children were still going about in their jerseys and short trousers, their ill-fitting shoes covered by moggins due to excessive wear. These gave them some sort of protection against the snow and cold; this was the seering hardship, (or torture) with which the poor and impoverished were stigmatised. The opulent, arrogant and the "respectable" classes, on the whole, regarded us as a lazy, shiftless lot, that had neither pride, energy nor brains to get out of a rut. We people of the hovels and the streets provided a rich field for the pent up consciences of the "do-gooders"! Nevertheless, we sometimes felt the benefit and warmth of those real Christian servants who really practised the loving care of our Lord Jesus. Hebron Hall in Thistle Street, The Band of Hope at Bon Accord Terrace or The Academy Hall in Academy Street all opened their doors to us young savages, ("The Street Arabs"), ("The Great Unwashed"). Even the very fact of my growing up could now be regarded as an overdue obituary for their great Christian work.

The long, dark, stormy nights were fast giving way to ever-increasing sunny hours, and the warm winds of Easter. Soon it was time to visit the Victoria, or Westburn Parks, where we congregated for the great ritual of rolling hard boiled eggs; each dyed with one of the colours of Joseph's coat. This event, to all the parents, appeared to be an oasis of joy and togetherness. Who can gauge, or value its significance in our young lives? This was the picnic when most adults managed to find the extra treat.

After extracting the last ounce of fun; rolling and smashing the eggshells to uncover the delicacy and eat it up, we enjoyed our simple games, playing with each other and receiving an extra fancy biscuit. Sometimes we got a cup of fizzy lemon to finish off the day's activity. Then like the plooboy, wended our way homewards as the sun's shadows grew longer; time to wash ourselves then be bundled off to bed, excited by the happy hours of being together, but Mother Nature and "The Japanese Sandman" took over, and soon we were fast asleep.

Counting Rhyme

"Eenery, feenerty, fickery, fae;
ell, del, dolman, eh :
irky, birky, stole an' rock;
an, tan, too is Jock."

The only thing we had in abundance was Imagination and Adventure. We were always looking for the pot of gold; and one way, so we thought, to ensure success, would be to climb into derelict houses and dig holes in the floors, or search the open, empty wallpresses, so convinced were we that we were on the right track. A little way down Minister Lane there was an open pend leading to such "treasure houses". I can tell you that we worked like beavers, but for all our labours, we only grew rich in knocks to our bodies, legs, chapped fingers or taes. One of us still managed to get his head stuck between the iron railings; panic stations, but it took an hour to get him freed.

Even with all these drawbacks surrounding "the crock of gold", we were never convinced that we were on a loser.

We made up quite a list on entertaining games to pass our free time, and most of us could take part in the games. One particular was "Put and Take", a brass top which you had to spin to find out if you had won a prize, or add to the kitty, and we helped to "ca" the ropes for the quines who were very expert in dodging in and out whilst we ca'ed the ropes. These girls had the skill and stamina to skip all day if necessary; but all the time, the spectre of going to school was fast approaching. The fact of Edward and Jeannie going to school never seemed to bother me; it was a world apart, but now it was beginning to become suddenly real and something that I couldn't dodge. Some of my pals were in the same boat, and they, like myself, were excited, yet afraid of this forthcoming and completely fresh event in our lives.

The great day arrived for me to start attending Skene Street School. Mum made sure that I was well scrubbed and shining like a golden sovereign to join the other scrubbed hopefuls, accompanied by their mums. One little boy in particular began bubbling and greeting; I remember him that day, lying down on a couch, scared out of his wits. His name, I found out was Robert Stevenson; he became a great pal of mine in the months ahead.

Rhyme

"Rise an' teem the pail Bel,
Rise an' teem the pail;
Oh Rise an' teem the pail Bel
Or I'll hae tae dee it masel."

Slop pails were once a familiar sight and required to be emptied regularly.

Sitting at her desk, dressed in black with a white lace collar was my first head teacher, Miss Isabella Leask, the infant mistress, and I thought that she was as old as the hills. To my young mind, nevertheless, she had the mien of a queen because she just commanded a special kind of obedience; she got it too. After satisfying Miss Leask with our crudentials, we were taken in hand by a Miss Marr, a nice, motherly grey-haired lady with her brightly coloured smock. I liked her straight away.

She then gathered her "brood", and we were shepherded into classroom 2, where we were each given a desk and seat. We had to give her our names and addresses, which she copied down into what appeared to me to be a big thick book — the school ledger. Suddenly, I just felt scared and alone, with the overwhelming feeling that I just wanted to get home to Mum. As I made a dash to the door, I was halted by a strong hand on my shoulder, and was gently steered to my desk, where I sat down and cried a little. Miss Marr gave me a friendly cuddle, wiped my face of my tears, then put her hand into her pocket; taking out a small bag of sweets, she popped one into my mouth, and as a result, the peace and confidence of one small boy was restored. I grew to like and respect this excellent teacher. Slates, and slate pencils followed, but we had to provide our own dusters. By the time a bell rang, we were all getting fidgetty; lo and behold, the mysteries and delights of playtime were revealed. It was all bewildering, meeting and mixing with so many new bairns. My sister and her pal Nellie Brand, who lived in Kidd Street, just round the corner from 2 Minister Lane, took me in hand to share their play-time piece; what a morale booster.

As the weeks passed by, we began to settle down to the daily routine and discipline. We also had a visit from the headmaster, Mr Alexander Moodie. He was a tall, elderly man, with grey hair and a receding hairline. I found him to be a friendly, kindly man; he told us that he considered lying, persistent bad conduct, and stealing to be "grave offences". Despite laying down the law, he took a personal interest in the welfare of individual pupils drawn from the poorer neighbourhoods. Every year, pupils from Skene Street won secondary school bursaries in open competition. Despite Mr Moodie's warnings, there were some distractions: A young boy, by the name of Bertram, was off school unwell. Nevertheless, he had the nerve to tricycle into our classroom, circled it, shouting "hello, hello". His antics were curtailed when he was caught inside the school premises by the janitor. I was sorry in a way that we never got a repeat performance.

Coloured pictures, I remember, were of assistance in our first venture to read and write; I also recall the screeching sound of our slate pencils upon our slates. Now and again, we got plasticine to make figures of anything we chose; it was an exercise which helped our little hands and minds develop a sense of co-ordination. This encouraged us to realise what it was like to reason out things for ourselves. The learning process was always boosted by Miss Marr with her bag of sweets to give one to the eager hands that were uplifted to give the right answer. I remember, with some regret, when one morning I hadn't a penny for playtime sweets, and it occurred to me that Mum was cleaning for Connon, the hairdresser at the top of Summer Street, (near Union Street). I thought that this could be an opportunity to get a penny. I waited until she opened the door to ask her for the penny so that I could go and buy sweeties at Knight the confectioner at the corner of Union Street and Summer Street. I did this, not knowing the hardships that I caused her; when I got them, they seemed to make a sour taste in my mouth. When you are young, you are never fussy how you get your pleasures; it was a lifetime lesson about being selfish, that I learned that day.

Sometimes my Father visited Mum at 2 Minister Lane, and then went out for the night. We huddled together until they came home. One night, we were in our next door neighbour's house, locked in, until they came home. All of a sudden, the door handle rattled. Some person was trying to push the door open. We were petrified, but never made a sound. Whoever it was, gave up, and then went away. I never had a further experience like that. An experience of a different nature was seeing for the first time, a well-known character by the name of Cakkie Appy, a small figure of a woman, often dressed in black. She appeared very old to us kids as we passed her by; it seemed that her face turned into a witch's face for our benefit. Certainly, her waspish manner scared the living daylights out of us. Whatever she may, or may not have been, her name is safe for posterity, while those who have been more benevolent to the city have passed into oblivion. We saw that fame is a precarious vocation.

Time and tide wait for no man; far less young people: The time had come when I had to move up a class at school. It hurt a lot to leave Miss Marr, for my time with her had made my childhood seem that lot sweeter and secure. There was compensation for me in store, for the teacher in Room 5 was Miss Elphinstone, a well-built woman, who I remember as having the traces of a burn mark on her face, but like Miss

Marr she had a heart of gold as well as a bag of sweeties. She must have been about fifty years of age, and she wore a belted green overall. I learned a lot in her class, and received my first bible certificate there. Mr Innes and his daughter, who ran a Sunday School in Calder's Dancing School in Summer Street, should take some of the credit for my success. After all, the Lord's word had fallen on fertile ground; there could be hope for some of the other little scamps to get civilised. Whilst I was in Room 5, there was a new boy drafted into the classroom. He had black curly hair, brown eyes and plumpish in build. He had a very nice manner and came from The Argentine. His name was Oliver, but that was all that I had gathered. He stayed a year in the classroom; a lifetime in my mind. It is funny how these happenings stick with you as your attitude to strangers begins to be more outward-looking. This was also the time when I sorted out my pals. They were Ross Hunter, who lived in Skene Street. I remember entering his house at the rear of the tenement, up stone stairs to three small attic rooms. Bobby Stevenson came from White House Street, but I was never in his house; why, I don't know; but more about him later.

This was my first real summer that I had ever played with steady pals. Most days were wiled away in never-ending adventures in "The Trainie Park", watching the trains go by. It was a great sight seeing the engines being put onto the turntable; a huge water tank and a leather sleeve feeding the rush of water into the boilers; something we could watch all day. The other great game we had was jumping into and playing in the granite enclosures with their iron grids to keep people from falling down a considerable depth. They were part of H.M. Theatre, and although we played many happy hours in them, we always had that dread of the iron grid breaking, to fall down into the deep shaft; never a happy thought, but the great enjoyment was the spinning of our tops. The first acquisition for spinning a top, was a type of whip. Most of us lads preferred a large band or headpiece rolled into a compact ensemble; a final tie in the centre, which made it keep its shape to whip up the top. We always judged the quality of the top with the number of rings around it. There were two types of tops: "Carrots" and "spinners". They each had their names, which included a "laird", a "lord", a "Lily", a "leaf", a "piper", a "drummer", a "hummer", a "thief". We spun our tops when we finished school until the growing shadows of night brought our efforts and fun to a close. It was great fun also to put various colours of chalk on the top of our tops, and when they were spinning, all the colours merged into a pattern that gave our

"tops" a touch of class and distinction. It is surprising that we did not erode the cement flagstones from the corner of "Little" Skene Street down to the Schoolhill station, but it gave an abundance of childish pleasure and a reservoir of happy memories to draw a measure of sustenance when the dark times need a little more strength to bear.

Another game which we young "gypes" played at was "trenchies", which necessitated an open ground with big boulders scattered around, with plenty of small stones to hand. Such a tract of ground lay between Skene Street and Skene Row. We "gypes" took cover behind the big boulders, with a pile of small stones beside us to throw at one another. On a Saturday forenoon we gathered on this waste ground to begin "The Battle of the Titans", puffed up with the British exploits against the Huns. We ducked behind our stone "trenches", and when the time was ripe to bob up and hurl our stones with force and accuracy for the discomfort of our enemies; during one of these battles I made a tactical mistake; I bobbed up too quick, and a stone exploded on my head; the blood gushed out, swamped over my neck to end up splashing my clothes. I instinctively plugged the wound to stem the flow of blood, then my pals took me home to Mum; I felt like a hero returning to base after doing feats of bravery. This feeling sustained me until I reached home. Mum was in, and when she saw me smirched with blood she nearly took a fit, but she didn't panic, and promptly pulled up a chair so that I could sit down. She produced a basin of cold water and a large cloth which she plunged into the basin without further ado to slosh it over my wound. I watched the water turn redder and redder as she continued this operation; not a squeak did she get out of me. When the blood had stopped oozing, she got a pair of scissors, and cut my hair back around the area of the wound. Finally she got a big piece of wadding, with a saturation of Iodine, (the "cure-all), placed it on the cut, then bandaged me up. I looked the part of a casualty from a battle ground, but for a repeat performance, I perished the thought. Glory can kill or disfigure.

There was always something to do for eager imaginations, zealous boys' minds, and mischievous hands . . . Well, we thought we could get some apples from one or two gardens not far from Kidd Street. A favourite spot was at Windsor Place, a small street with back gardens running between Thistle Lane and Victoria Street. This was our target, so the four of us ran up and spotted out the lie of the land for any dangers; not seeing any visible signs, we descended, like "wolves on the fold". We reached the tree unopposed, our hands upon the "forbidden fruit", when there was a loud crash of a closing door, and an irate owner rushed at us, using a lot of unintelligible language. We dropped everything and made a desperate dash to retreat the way we came in and just made it, breathless and scared from his avenging hand. After this rebuff, we made a few more "sorties" against well-known "targets", but the initial reverse sapped our will and enthusiasm. It was a relief to return to "base", and the thoughts of future apple-raiding plans folded like the tents of the Arabs as they silently steal away.

The rough and tumble of the playground divided us into two or three "factions": Many a bloody encounter was the means of settling disputes; yet I can never recollect any of these boys being a bully, or taking anything by force from any weaker boy. One afternoon, after school, Bobby Stevenson, Ross Hunter and I were acting the goat on the pavement outside Skene Street School, shouting and jumping upon one another, and generally rolling about. Suddenly, a stern female voice stopped us in our tracks; imagine our surprise, to see our headmistress, Miss Leask, shaking her fist, demanding us to cease forthwith. We received a verbal barrage about discipline on the street, and told to report to her study, first thing in the morning. It was like a sentence of being shot at dawn, and we wished that tomorrow would never come. The dreaded morning duly arrived, and we shuffled into her room like convicted criminals, and after a sound lecture, she asked why we were acting like "hooligans", as she put it. Ross and Bobby mumbled something inaudible, then remained silent. Something stirred inside me, and I surprised myself when I spoke up with indignation, vowing that it was "just fun", and "after all, nobody was hurt". It must have worked, for we were censured again, then sent back to our classrooms, giving sighs of relief. There is a saying, "once caught, twice shy"; that was true in our case.

Mum was very strict; once our homework had been attended to, that we were bedded by 7-7.30 p.m. There was no respite for her, after the hard, grinding daily tasks with their pitiful reward, for she had to catch up with her household chores, which took her far into the night, draining her strength so much that we were concerned about her health. This in fact prevented her from her usual work, resulting in less money to support us on a balanced, nutritious diet. Whatever that term meant. It was a mystery to me, for we got porridge, brose, soup, tatties, jammy pieces, and occasionally salt herring, red herring or smokies when they were cheap to buy; last but not least, fried bread.

The upshot was, that Edward and I had to get free meals, (breakfast and dinners) plus a glass of milk and a bun at playtime, under the supervision of Miss Leask. I thought it inexplicable being censured by this school "goddess" on one occasion, and the next time being your "handmaiden". It is said that gold is more valuable when purified through the fiery furnace of experience.

The routine of going down to Trinity Church Hall, Shoe Lane, for our breakfast at 8 a.m., and down there again for our dinners at 12-30 p.m., five days a week in all kinds of weather was an episode in our young lives that needed courage and stamina in no small measure. These journeys, often as not, were plagued with problems, and often involved personal violence from some older bullies that attended free meals; it was like running the gauntlet of fear, with all its nasty incidents: bullying, the discipline hardship of authority that doled out our bread of life. The too scanty clothing that we wore during the winter scene, that was all too unsuitable to keep us warm; the chapped fingers, the chilblains, wet feet, the stinging ears, the running noses, the chest colds, all endured in the name of "Christian Charity".

Our daily journey to Shoe Lane started by getting up from a warm bed into a cold, frosty room. Whenever you breathed out, your frozen breath hung like small clouds in the room. You hurriedly pulled on your trousers, hitched up with galasses, then on with the jersey with its visible signs of wear and tear; the woollen pair of socks that came up to my knees followed, and I fixed them in place with a piece of elastic, pulling on my "parish pair of tacketty beets", tied up with leather thongs. I braced myself to fill up the basin with cold water from the ewer, splashing the water over my face to just give it a "cat's lick". Once I had parted my hair into a middle shade, I was all set, ready to go. One ritual left before leaving the house was the kiss of a loving Mum.

I ran down the stone stairs into Minister Lane, then round to Kidd Street, where I met two or three more lads, who like myself were the innocent victims of our environment. I won't name the other boys, because we all had the same surname, "Poverty". Some of us were a little more fortunate, but we all had the same place to go to, "Trinity Church Hall", Shoe Lane, in order to tide us over for another day. After a bit of horse play, we imagined that we were cowboys, just like W. S. Hart, Hoot Gibson and others as we galloped along Kidd Street to cross Summer Street. We made a mad dash down the steep slope of Skene Terrace, past the "Picture Drome"; then headed up the spur road into Rosemount Viaduct, with "The Trainie Parkie" on our right, slowing up as we passed by the construction works in progress at the War Memorial, when the granite Lion was put in situ one day outside The Cowdray Hall. We then sped past Robert Gordon's College at the double then on to my favourite stretch of the road, Schoolhill, Back Wynd and Harriet Street. I have always had a feeling about St. Nicholas Church. It represents something ageless, warm and expressive of life and people to my mind. As we ran past the jeweller's shop on the corner into St. Nicholas Street itself, we could see our reflections in the big mirror of Reid & Pearson's big store, before we left the main thoroughfare to puff up Flourmill Brae past The Dispensary, cutting our way through some partially demolished houses onto The Guestrow itself. We called this narrow thoroughfare, "The Gush". The cobbled stone street was littered with filth and pools of clarty water dispersed throughout the length of this byeway from an earlier age of more illustrious civic history. Once we had passed over this lot, we nipped down Ragg's Lane, and on to Broad Street which was paved with wooden blocks instead of the slippery stone setts. The last lap of the journey was Queen Street with the granite filigree work of Greyfriars Church tower on the corner. Not far down, on the left hand side, almost opposite the entrance to Lodge Walk, was Shoe Lane itself, where we made a final frantic dash past the dingy row of long worn-out buildings also ripe for demolition.

As we arrived at the Church Hall, there were many like us, waiting to get in. The man who opened the door was a stocky, elderly man, with a moustache. He was dressed in a janitor's uniform, and reminded us of the procedure before entering the hall. There were two boards hung up, which assisted them in their attempts to regiment us. One was full of wooden pegs that fitted into numbers on the board; one of which was allocated to you. On the way in, you were required to pull out your number peg and put it into the corresponding hole for your number on the adjacent board. Inside the hall, were long wooden tables, with wooden forms alongside them. Three or four women wearing white uniforms and caps dished up the food in enamel bowls. In the morning it was porridge and milk. Sometimes it was burnt, but you had to eat it up, for no leftovers were allowed. Mr Mathieson, the janitor, made certain that there was no nonsense with us lot; he was a tough old nut, but fair. We went through the same old performance at dinner time: Soup, pudding, milk and

bread, (the same rules applying to leftovers), but sometimes the pudding, too, was burnt, and it took a strong stomach and resolution with which to comply. During that time we went to Shoe Lane daily; there was a big lad who followed us down the way with the intent of bullying and interfering with us. This made the journey a real terror trail. Many a time he stopped me and disparagingly called me "Chinky", or other names. It didn't worry me untoward because I kent that he came from Richmond Street, and was unsociable to others. Then one day he just disappeared . . . Life was a lot better after that, but there was an occasion when I was on my way to school after my breakfast at Trinity Hall. It was a real sunny morning, but a bit on the chilly side, when I had crossed Broad Street from Marischal College and was nearing the corner of Upper Kirkgate, when I heard a clumping noise every few seconds approaching me . . . Round the corner, a few yards ahead of me was a young man, or rather half of a man fixed on a two inch square block of wood. He was propelling himself forward by means of his hands which were encased in khaki mittens. He also had on a khaki pullover with a cloth cap on his head. I stood and watched him as he clomped his way past, and disappeared up The Gallowgate. I have often wondered where he had to go in order to survive with his mutilated body. I surmised that he may have been a war victim on account of his khaki clothing. One thing was certain, he made a lasting impression upon my mind, and later on in life when I commenced reading Shakespeare, I found one verse which the bard had written which struck me as being highly appropriate: "Seeking the bubble of reputation, even at the cannon's mouth". Maybe this was the key to it all. Somehow or other, that passing horror changed something inside me about the relative values of violence.

In our congested rookery of back streets, illness was a common occurrence amongst us, and of course there were the times of childbirth, and little facilities or money whereby the doctors could be paid. There was lack of creature comforts to make the patients well again soon. There seemed an interminable end to the same old problems and hardships. The seemingly unnoticed backwash of little hope or less future, unseen by outside eyes. Yet here, still walked the faint footsteps of Christ's teaching and love, for in our midst, two old females were on call to help in our emergencies, to take over the midnight or daily vigil; to look after the sick bed, or help with humble chores in addition to caring for the children when tragedy struck, often without warning. Yet nobody could take our humour from us. Often it was a rough-edged barb that sometimes eased tensions, to give hope when despair was the only answer; ours was a gutsy, earthy and sometimes blasphemous repartee. Perchance Heaven intruded, for according to framed biblical texts in illuminated lettering, "The Lord will provide": We never are entirely forgotten.

It is a sad moment in life when you lose your hero; maybe he is a boy three of four years older than yourself. In my case he was the football hero of my school and my strongest pal; defender of "The Small Fry" at Skene Street School, and on home territory "The Cock of the Walk" in Kidd Street.

We younger lads in the street saw something in Jimmy Gordon that made us feel good because he mixed with our company, taught us many games, and to play them fairly. He stayed with his grandmother; she was a sort of recluse. She wore black dresses, and a long black shawl, but gave what she could when trouble erupted around us. I remember one evening that I woke up suddenly and heard quite a few people on the move, but voices were very subdued. Mum was preparing to go out, and when I asked her where she was going, she told me to go back to sleep, remaining tight-lipped about what had occurred that necessitated her going out at that late hour. I found it difficult to get back to sleep, but upon my waking up when morning came, Mum was there to take me in her arms and she gently told me that Jimmy Gordon had died during the night with consumption. It seemed so unlikely that our Jimmy could go like that; our pal that we so admired; trusted so much . . . gone. It began to penetrate my mind that it must be true. Somehow I was so choked up with a sense of loss that I just couldn't cry. Mum and the rest of the women folk looked after Mrs Gordon, trying to comfort her in so many ways that they felt that they could help; but when you lose your only, and much-loved grandson at that tender age who gave her a reason to live even in these squalid conditions, the women folk even were unable to administer a single crumb of comfort; Mrs Gordon had become over-taxed, mentally and emotionally. In no time she just seemed to disappear; wherever it may have been, I never knew, but Jimmy has always retained his niche in my memory.

Counting Rhyme

"Eeenery, twaaery, tuckery tayven;
Halba, crackery, ten or elayven:
Peen, pan, musky, dam,
Feedelam, eadelam, twenty one."

As the nights darkened, they brought closer the celebration and ritual of Hallowe'en; to us it was a time of "aippledooking", "treacle aipplies", "Chinese Lanterns" and "Knackies", (or turnips), hollowed out, complete with eyes and a mouth, with a candle inserted in them in order that we might visit the various houses at night. It was a thought, present in our minds, that witches lurked in dark places, and that our lanterns could chase them out.

Chinese lanterns were popular with us, but in a way they were a fire hazard. They were made of paper, with their small, lighted candles inside, and if you hadn't a steady hand, the candle became upset, falling against the paper cover and burst into flame. Many of us experienced this form of burn, and quite a few carry their scars to the present day. Hallowe'en was quickly followed by Guy Fawke's Night, and I can say that there little in the way of fireworks show where we stayed, but of course there was a bonfire of odds and ends in our back green, but it didn't lack in enthusiasm however modest it may have been as we all linked hands. Only a few days prior to this event, we had tapped what we considered was a bottomless well of wealth garnered from generous people in Kidd Street where there was three shillings and sixpence in pickings, accompanied by a lot of banter, including retorts like "begging buggars", or "bloody scruff", but we could take their jibes, "nae bother . . .", for when our few fireworks had gone we all agreed that it had been worth all the abuse that we had borne.

Even as a child I could detect folk's ill-flawed attitudes. Envy, greed and grandeur bogged down any spiritual feelings that they might have had; our civilisation had drifted far from the real state of things. My heart felt a chill as I wondered what the outcome of their anti-Christ philosophy would be in after years.

With Hallowe'en and Guy Fawkes departing into the past, and Christmas not far off, we started thinking about Christmas stockings, "clootie dumplings", and all the other perks for our kind of people. Well, we knew that we would get something, however little; our credit with the tuck shop was maybe a little shaky, but it would see us through, and that was a godsend; but there was a little extra going for us: Edward was doing a milk round at this time, which meant he got three shillings per week for starting at 5 a.m. until 7.30 a.m., seven days a week. There was an added attraction, because it was the West End that he covered on his round, and he could "scran the buckets" in the "wee sma' 'oors". It was surprising what these people would throw away, and it might make the difference for us between a dry loaf Christmas, and one in which we could indulge in the love and excitement of Christmas family gatherings. Gatherings which were all too rare throughout the rest of the year. A week before Christmas, I knew that our fortunes were about to improve. Edward had saved all his tips, which amounted to £3.00. A week before Christmas, we had successfully salvaged hardly used toys, and other useful articles, which we sold for a few shillings. Yes, this was indeed "corn in Egypt", when we bought some Christmas fare from Forbes Stuart (Italian Warehouse) in Huntly Street. We knew that we would have a good time within the scope of our purse, but the nagging thought behind our minds was what some of the poor sods of our neighbours' families, those "poor buggers" would receive; suffering time and time again the indignity of being totally poor, with not even a Christmas decoration between them to bring a little Christmas cheer amid the dimmed gas, candle or paraffin light of their homes. It was a passable, merry Christmas for a few of us, but as the New Year came nearer, I believe that the good Lord never fore-closes his mercy to his children; quite a few of us had invitations to a New Year treat in the Picture House, where we got a bag of cakes, a bag of chocolate candies, an orange, an apple and a free show. To add to that, Mum shared out a lot of goodies that we had managed to get by our stroke of good fortune. At least we had survived another year. If the winter is rainy or snowy, that is the time we would saturate the outside of our boots with fish oil or grease; if you wanted dry feet, this was one way of doing it.

I became friendly with some of the boys from The Hard-weird, and I often played with two or three of them on the stone staircase that ran down from Skene Street to the Knight Templa's wallie at the bottom. I always got a cold sensitive feeling when I sat down inside the well. The spring must have dried up maybe at the time South Mount Street was constructed. At the top of the stairs was the single storey shop of Styles the barber, who also had an assistant; I always got my hair cropped there at fourpence a time. The assistant was a great Rangers' enthusiast, and the tales of greatness associated with players such as McRobb, (goalkeeper), McPhail, (inside left), and Alex. Martin, (in his opinion the greatest outside left), never ceased to amaze me. From all the insight into the players' tactics, I should have been a rabid Rangers' fan, but the feeling never accompanied me from the shop; nevertheless I enjoyed it while he was cutting my hair.

The Hardweird that I knew at this time was partially demolished, but there were a few houses still standing, if that is the appropriate word. The means of entrance being the forestairs that led up to the front doors. Washing was always festooning the banisters, which often as not, were missing the occasional cast iron spar. Small bairns with a beseeching look in their eyes stuck their head and shoulders through such gaps, as any stranger approached. Their young mothers looked prematurely haggard and worn, with their "shawlies" wrapped closely around them. This was a moment in time that my young mind perceived the acid difference of being poor, and knowing how poor can other people get. The answer for me was found in The Hardweird, in this ailing, ancient pile of mortar and stones, harbouring inside them human beings huddled together in dark holes described as "rooms". When you saw the children, some of them without proper clothing, accustomed to running around bare-footed, irrespective of the conditions of the ground, which was very rough, broken up, and strewn with all kinds of stones. Many a case of Scarlet Fever, Diptheria, scabs, immaciation and affliction by Rickets was noticed in its early stages by the teachers of the classes that they attended at Skene Street School nearby. In the class-rooms there was always a lingering smell of paraffin, a sure sign of lice. These people did their very best to keep above the level of their degredation, but unemployment, overcrowding, lack of sometimes the barest facilities like toilets, washing spaces, and running water to supply their hygienic needs was in many cases ignored by the parish authorities. In fact these people would have had a better life in The Poors House, but in there, they could in time be broken up as a family, and scattered all over the county in foster-parent homes, to lose touch with one another. In my experience, these families, despite their misfortunes and poverty, were a warm, close-knit people with a sturdy independence that would give a helping hand to the underdog, and my pals from The Hardweird would share out what they had; I liked the way that they gave. Nobody from outwith the clan seemed on the face of it to care what happened to them yet they were as chirpy as sparrows. Although their legs were caught in the mantrap of our immoral civilisation, they saw no need to sever their connections with The Hardweird. The stream of life that they hailed from didn't require that kind of streak, or person-ality trait, that the world knows as "viciousness".

Just before The Hardweird joins Jack's Brae, there stands a corporation urinal. It is not a mystery now to me why it was put there; I still wonder if it drained into The Denburn, our most famous "underground river".

Up from The Hardweird is the steep slope of Jack's Brae, lined by similar looking houses as The Denburn. Most mornings, those trudging up Jack's Brae could see the wooden wheelbarrow of Jimmy The Scaffie standing near the pavement's edge. Upon reaching Blair's Lane, a dark entry, the spare figure of Mrs Findlay could be spotted flitting about restlessly intent on her chores; some children thought that she was the resident ghost . . . Other worthies were known by simple names such as "The Poacher", who bade at No. 21, doon a closie. He belonged to the flesh and blood brigade: When he washed his face, nosy quines would ask him where he was going? Another individual was "Simon The Russian". "Umbrella Johnston" was a tall, thin mannie. Folk were amazed that a "gust o' win'" didn't blow him "doon tae the green". At the crest of the Brae was the meeting place of wifies in black shawls enjoying a "claikin' session", "spiering aboot and scandalising onybody an' abody"; Mary Nichol's parrot wasn't always a silent witness. A penniless mild cratur went about with an empty purse asking if "onybody could change a quid".

In March Lane, a classmate of mine, Billy Houston, lived with his sister Helen. I also heard of the small shoppie that sold red candy and toffee; the colour of the candy being a dye extract from our exercise book covers which were boiled up when the proprietor could get them on "The Black Market". I never went near this shoppie to find out, (and I'm nae gingin' back).

When winter's "snaw fell thick an' saft", Jack's Brae came into its own. It was the mecca for every type of sledge, and the price they paid for their pleasure was cracked and split skulls, and in the morning, The Broadford Bell called the mill workers to work. If anybody was late, the gates were closed and a day's pay was forfeited; you had to pay for your sins.

"Swine's Closie" was another road running from Skene Street, alongside Skene Street School, down the brae, to enter The Hardweird and Jack's Brae. There were two houses off this closie which were always a source of curiosity and mystery to me; who lived there? Like a lot of the "aul' hoosies", they are gone and their lairach's grassed over. Swine's Close got its name, because when it was farmland, some of the local crofters drove their herds down this path to The Denburn. Over the other side of The Denburn to The Hardweird, can be found the remnants of Stevenson Street, once the main thoroughfare from the Rosemount district into the city. Now it gives an outward impression that it is merely a spur road, and a cul-de-sac off Leadside Road.

Though the tenements are more substantial than the hovels of Jack's Brae and The Hardweird, it was a dark, mean street, with hallways like dark tunnels; ricketty, well-worn lobbies, staircases and landings. If there was any illumination at night, it was provided by little oil lamps hung outside the doors. Here it seemed that "ye were awa' back in the days o' the 'cruisie' (rush wick lights), and widden bilers". Facilities of the meanest nature were their strong point; the W.C.'s were ochre-daubed boxes with uncertain plumbing, but we had a liberal supply of cut-up "Evening Expresses"; an essential "must" for overcrowded families.

Stevenson Street had its pretensions, with the Mission Hall and Pawnshop and just across the road was a building where the washing was done. Two or three "sma' shoppies" supplied the humble needs of the neighbourhood.

Further up Denburn was a small lane, named Garden Neuk Close. The sound of its name gave the street an air of gentility, but this was not so. It was just a tumble-down replica of The Denburn. Lackie Thomson stabled his horses there and hired them out to The Territorial Army Scottish Horse in Ruby Lane Barracks. Trail, the other horse dealer, also had his stables in The Denburn. The Denburn and Jack's Brae area was a capital parade square where the town horses could be seen at close quarters. The shortening days and long, dark evenings meant that we were increasingly confined at home; homework being the priority. There were two or three opportunities that broke the boring uniformity of the winter evenings. At school, where I was sticking into my lessons, and paying attention to the lessons that my beloved teacher, Miss Elphinstone, was imparting, I attained an above-average mark on my record card. There was a directive from the headmaster for our teacher to pick some of her pupils for a lecture by G. M. Fraser, the City Librarian, who was to address us with a lecture on the history of Aberdeen; we were then to write an essay afterwards.

I was one of the few that attended this lecture in the Headquarters at the bottom of "Little Skene Street", where I noticed for the first time that there was a narrow, steep, stone stair leading from the rear of the library up to H. M. Theatre. When we were all seated in the lecture room and reasonably quiet, G. M. Fraser entered the room, and I was immediately impressed with his looks and bearing. When he began his lecture on the history of our city, his erudition and eloquence which he deployed in describing the changing face of Aberdeen through the centuries, its civic and economic ups and downs as well as the part played by successive generations of local families, fired my imagination.

The first encounter with G. M. Fraser has made me a confirmed admirer and reader of this brilliant librarian and author. Even then, I felt the deep pride and faith that he had in the continuing welfare and progress of his city; the concern which he had that the assets and beauty should be allowed to endure. With all this zeal and admiration that I acquired at this, my first formal lecture, the essay that I wrote failed to win a prize; but I won something else: a respect and feeling for my city, and the efforts that it had made to better and uplift the less fortunate families, so that they weren't chained to poverty and its consequences for ever. The genuine Aberdonian has always strived to banish this spectre from our community. Political parties may come and go; Local Government institutions may be subject to repeated reorganisation, but the Aberdonian has no change of heart. A beautiful observation from Gray's Elegy can be refuted when one hears a master like G. M. Fraser. I found that the city in bloom lay within my compass points after all, that no thinking mind should make itself prey to canker or be "a rose that is born to blush unseen, and waste its sweetness in the desert air". I would lay claim to my city through the written word.

The other occasion that gave us a pleasurable and instructable night as prospective Christian socialists was when we were invited out to The Hebron Hall in Thistle Street, where we enjoyed a lantern show which depicted stories from The New Testament. All these pursuits of our young lives weaned us towards more mature living, and thinking.

The early months of the year with their usual spates of changeable weather was having a weakening effect upon my Mum. It was more noticeable than ever before. It prevented her from tackling any employment, however humble, and it did not surprise me when she took us together with tears in her eyes and told us that she could not pay the rent so we would have to move from Minister Lane. However, within the week, she had got us a room in St. Andrew Street, through a friend of Dad's who was in the painting trade. This man would be our new landlord.

Whilst we were at school, Dad, and a mate who had a "cairtie", flitted the few bits and pieces to our next house. As a young boy, I had felt that my grass roots had been torn out: The suddenness of this move created excitement, doubling up the fear of leaving familiar places and pals. The essence was an overwhelming sense of loss. I remember eagerly promising pals that I would return and play together with them as I had usually done. Time does tell that this seldom happens.

I remember going down with Mum and the family to our new abode. It was situated at the corner of Crooked Lane and St. Andrew Street. The front of the tenement had a dirty grey appearance. There was an Italian shop next door. To enter, we had to go down a steep stone staircase, along a cobbled paving towards the entrance of the tenement which had been there since the "Burking days"; the anatomy theatre had stood not far away until it was destroyed by a mob of irate townspeople from the East End. Our entry looked like the all-too-familiar "Black Hole of Calcutta". The winding staircase took us up to our first floor room, and there was a small sink with a brass tap en route. It glinted through the gloom seemingly like a miracle. When Mum opened the door, we entered two gloomy rooms which were not very big. The wallpaper was tattered in places, and there were signs of dampness, and I knew that there would be bugs. There was also a small fireplace, but no gas light or ring. Everything would have to be cooked upon the fire.

Dad and his friend had already placed our possessions in situ. The two beds, one at the side of the front window, and my bed at the back of the door; the ogee chest at the end of my bed, and our table in front of the window. Our only means of illumination was the paraffin lamp. In the back room, there was a press door which was locked, and I saw two white mice come out of a hole at the side, looking for titbits, which gave us pleasure to see them, and they turned out to be very tame.

The back window looked on to a wasteground with a wooden "gibbet", and beyond that was a very small pub named "The Oddfellows" on Crooked Lane.

Opposite that establishment was a corporation urinal inside the wall which tagged onto the wall which enclosed Robert Gordon's College. That ancient pile of learning always fascinated me, when I looked through the iron gates towards the huge bastion-like edifice; its imposing appearance far removed from our way of life.

In a way, we had just changed addresses; the slum conditions may have been slightly worse: no gaslight; but the sink on the stairs balanced the odds. When we went to St. Andrew Street, it meant that we would have to leave Skene Street School and enrol on the books of the school nearest to us, which was in our case "The Demonstration School", Charlotte Street. I presented myself at the school, and was amongst the many other pupils who were being sorted out, and when it came to my turn, they had a confab, then they told me that I could go back to Skene Street right away.

Apparently I wasn't on their list. This gave me the feeling that I was "the prodigal son", when I returned to my classroom. All's well, that ends well . . . "The Living In" experience was all that I had had, though it was to be a continuing fight against dampness and the biting bugs. Occasionally I was attacked by "flechs" with equal ferocity.

All this way of life was the lot of a countless number of families. I sifted through my mind continually, the inheritance of social insignificance of these people, whilst I was playing on my own. After a few days, some of the boys in the next tenement, and others from across the street, began to speak to me, and in no time we became friends and exchanged names and information regarding ourselves and our families. Our way, in which we combatted the problems of the world, was to foregather by the corner shop at the junction of Charlotte and St. Andrew Street and spin yarns about our impossible dreams or ambitions. We got a lot of pleasure out of it, except when the shop lights went out, and we had to return home to reality; the same trivial round. It was rather strange to me though going "home" to St. Andrew Street, rather than Minister Lane. My regular route now was up The Denburn, past Black's Buildings and on to Woolmanhill. Then up a little bit turning into St. Andrew Street past the hospital. The only exception to this routine was on the Friday afternoon when the school closed. Then I went along Skene Street, on to Rosemount Viaduct, then keeked over the granite balustrades on Union Terrace, where I saw a lot of farm servants standing in cliques, engaged in serious conversations. Some had consumed too much whisky and were capering about, "cha'ing the fat" with one another. Friday and Saturday in town was their well-earned break from the confined, hard-graft living on the farm. Most of them were dressed in blue suits, big cloth caps, drain pipe trousers and shiny black boots, and smoking their short-stemmed pipes. I always had a respect for these men of the soil, for their roots were my roots originally. Aberdeen's distinction, growth and qualities were continually replenished when they settled and worked in our city over the passing generations. Their joys were simple: a night amongst the stalls in "The Castler"; the "try your strength machines" which were always rigged to encourage rivalry or competition, were a highlight of the evening, as well as the various bars around The Castlegate. Then came the rush to catch the last bus or train home, but some of them never did manage to do that . . . The army had a smartly-dressed sergeant in the regimental uniform walking round The Castlegate seeking recruits. He painted a bright picture of army life; the security of employment, the adventure besides; serving of King and Country. His descriptive powers did bring in plenty of recruits, and the first night of their army life began in The Castlehill Barracks.

Saturday at The Castlegate was the "hub" of the city for local and rural visitors. Here was gathered the quick pound salesman, with the showy trashy goods. The electric machine man, who sold electric shocks; Bronco the coloured gent who pulled teeth with his fingers. Mr Troup with his fruit stall alongside, was the gentleman who sold shillingie bags of various fruit. Another of the same ilk included in his bags, broken slabs of Duncan's chocolate. In a small corner of the market stood a dark-skinned man, dressed in a blue robe, with a blue and gold cap on his head. He sold his fortunes amid burning sticks of incense. Last, but not least, was "Dante", who sold contraceptives, and "the elixir of life", a cure-all for any malady.

I was just short of nine years of age, and still in Mr Smith's class in Room 15 at Skene Street School, and living at St. Andrew Street meant that I was cut off from any of my school pals after lessons were over. This was made up for by a more continuing closeness with my new-found friends at St. Andrew Street, who were more subdued in their feelings and approach than the more boisterous and devil-may-care intentions of my school pals. In a way, this quieter environment made me aware of the dangers that a young lad could be living in, and unaware of its presence actually walking around with you. I noticed that when we were playing around that there was always a bloke, probably twenty-five years of age, hanging around. He was thin-faced, sharp-nosed and his eyes were "fishy". His clothes were ill-fitting, and his shoes worn down. He was muffled up with a dirty thick scarf, and wore an equally filthy cloth cap. His mode of walking was a sort of shuffle, with his head bent down, and his hands deep in his seemingly cavernous pockets. I always felt apprehensive as he shuffled past us, weighing us all up in a manner that was scary and repulsive.

Our W.C. was just off the main passage behind the tenement. There were four cubicles, and ours was the last one. The W.C.'s ran parallel to the entrance passage; it was quite dark, with only some borrowed light from a small window. It was after coming home from school one day when Mum wasn't in, that I went downstairs, and through the dark entry intent on playing with two other boys. I had to go to the toilet on the way; when I went inside, someone gripped my arms in a tight vice. A voice, thick with emotion hissed in my ear "Dinna shout and ye won't be hurt," and at the same time, a man tried to push coins into my hand.

I don't know how I didn't panic at that moment, but I just galvanised into action, which put the man off balance against the pipes. By sheer instinct, I lashed out at his legs with my heavy tacketty boots, and I must have got him in a very tender spot, because he came out with a terrible roar of pain, and collapsed over the pot. This was my opportunity to make a dash for safety, and my feet went like the hammers of hell on to the street. I disappeared behind a shop door, and after about ten minutes, I saw this creep, emerging into the street and he was nearly crying with rage and pain. He looked round, trying to spot me, but failing, he hobbled away down the street. I hope that it may have taught him a moral lesson.

After that nasty experience with that immoral creep, who hung around young people just like a bird of prey on the lookout for a fledgling to fall out of the nest, it taught me to be cautious with more adult people; these sort of people come in many disguises.

I met in with two brothers who stayed in the big tenement at the corner of the street opposite Isaac Benzies' store. This building was more superior to our down-at-heel abodes. They were different from the other boys that I had previously played with; they were always visiting another part of town. I remember during a school holiday that they were keen to visit The Regent Quay, and they asked me to come along. I agreed like a shot, it being a warm and sunny afternoon. Our first stop was at the confectioners to look into the window and see if we could buy any sweets. Whilst standing outside, I started to play with a small magnifying glass that I was carrying with me, and used it to start burning pieces of paper by directing the heat of the sun through the glass. We were all engrossed in this way when a man's voice said "Can ye licht my pipe wi' yer glaiss?" We could, and we would. We were very proud loons when we saw the smoke curling out of his pipe to his satisfaction, and we were rewarded with the welcome sum of twopence which we divided, to blow on a bar of "Five Boys" chocolate. After this windfall, we ran down George Street past the Soup Kitchen into Loch Street, then past Greigie's the toffee and boiled sweet confectioners; turning sharp right into Drum's Lane, a dirty narrow street lined with squalid buildings, straight through into The Upperkirkgate. We crossed over into "The Gush", (Guestrow), and sped on to The Netherkirkgate, without stopping to explore the courts that led off our straight and narrow route to The Castlegate. We decided to go down to Virginia Street by way of Castle Terrace via "The Hangman's Brae Staircase".

Virginia Street to me, was long and brooding, with a grey kind of atmosphere, dominated by the flyover bridge which provided Marischal Street access to Regent Quay. On the side opposite the steps up from Virginia Street to "Bannerman's Brig" were a number of streets running parallel to each other, back in the direction of Commerce Street. These are Mearns Street, Water Lane, James Street and Sugarhouse Lane, the former slum areas of The Shorelands. I had heard stories of the overcrowding misery there, but as we came nearer the Harbour, it was thrilling and exciting to see all these iron ships moored alongside the quay, tied to iron bollards with thick ropes; their different coloured hulls and proud profiles rivetted our attention. We followed the line of ships along an open-planked wooden platform, and could see and hear the lapping of the waters underneath. Another sight that we delighted in was the round piles of thick, brown, tarry and creosote-smelling ropes. To me a true smell of ship, sea and sailor: The far-off smell of a bygone past. When we reached the end of the wooden platform, we looked down at the heaving waters sluishing around the cement bulwark and saw quite a number of small fishes swimming around. Like the boys that James McBey depicted in his etching of such a scene, we must have stayed watching and pelting these fish with anything that we could find for at least two hours. Even then, we were reluctant to go away, but time was pressing, so we returned to Virginia Street by way of Shore Lane, past its old storage buildings. Then we came across the horses and cairts of the Shore Porters Society at work, all kinds of goods being handled by strong, horny-handed men who appeared like Hercules to us. As we walked by admiring this great show of industry and commerce, one of these cairters gave me a "handfay" of locust beans; what a rare treat. We then passed under the brig, and went in the opposite direction, past Theatre Lane to Weigh House Square, where storage was also available for all sorts of merchandise. These operations were undertaken by the cairters of Mutter & Howie, who had another depot in Charlotte Street not far from my home.

The Weigh House was a personal disaster to my family: our grandfather was fatally injured there during his working hours when part of the crane fell on his head; his body being trundled home in an open cairt, shrouded by an old tarpaulin. Somehow being here seemed to possess my whole mind with what psychics describe as a sense of "deja-vu". Without a word, I turned my back on my pals, and scooted homewards away from it all; the last time to be in their company.

When life is going not too bad, things take a turn for the worse. My sister Georgina suddenly went down ill with an attack of the "flu" as Mum thought, and she lay in bed for a few days suffering worsening headaches. When I came home from school one day, Georgina had been taken to Cunninger Hill Hospital, which to us was a much-feared place. I mind, one night, when we were all in bed, a knock on the door; when Mum answered it, a policeman was standing there. Something was said, and Mum, who was shaking, came through and put on her clothes without saying anything. It must have been very late at night when she returned and woke us all up. It was an awful experience to me when Mum, who could hardly control herself with her grief and distress, gathered us all together to tell us that our sister had died in hospital. We later knew that it was Meningitis that she had been ill with, and that her constitution had not been sufficiently strong to combat it. This was my first experience of tragedy within the family unit.

Faith

Dinna fash or greet aboot oorsels;
God's licht disnae dim — the lampie is aye fu'.
Oor laird, if in oor herts gies muckle joy;
His kist gies us meat an' ale — we nivver wint.
His werdies (cam' fit mae) they will aye-wyes ding,
Fit ere a warld o' doot or feer dirls in oor lugs.

FIT-LIKE, BILLIES

I aften winder if there is a maister plooman apairt frae man:—
We micht only be a speckie chaff in the chaumer o' time.
Weer aye speerin' tae ane anither fu' we bide in the same hoose —
It aye seems whirlin' an' rooshin' aroon a' ba' o' fire; we a' ken ane
anither, bit nae at weel . . .
We a' jist chauve awa' deein' oor ain thing; the guid an' the deil hae
their wye in oor herts — (the giftie tae unnerstan'); but we are gey thraan
folkies an' canna' mak' up oor minds — jist fechtin' an' girnin' amang
oorsels — we hae a puckle sense, but we get tapsilteerie in oor heid: It is
fan' I tak' a fearin' to hae a stracht line, to ken far I am gyan.

Not long after this, when leaving for school, I was a wee bit late, so began running towards Woolmanhill when I noticed an empty tin can lying on the pavement. I couldn't help kicking it, for after all, it would keep me running all the way, so that I would be on time for school. I began to think that I was an international player like Alan Morton, and I duly dribbled and wove the tin like a ball. I smacked it across Woolmanhill, towards Black's Buildings, and as I approached the corner of the playground attached to the hospital, I dribbled the tin to the edge of the pavement and kicked it into the roadway. I must have caught my toecap on an upraised stone, and went flying on to my back on the cassies. As I tried to rise, a Scotch terrier and a larger dog attacked me with tooth and claw and seemed to be getting the upper hand, despite my shouting for help. I was hitting out vigorously, and despite the pain, I was holding on, when a man drove them off, and I was safe. I owe a lot to that brave man as I was helped across to the chemist's shop. The chemist himself and girl assistant helped to bandage me up without payment, and got me to The Sick Children's Hospital in the Castle Terrace, where I got an injection and my bruises and weals attended to. I had to make my own way home. A good job that Mum was there, and without fuss she put me to bed. I needed my bed, as I was shaken up, in pain, and tired. On the second night a woman came to our home. She said that she was the owner of one of the dogs, and had come to see how I was getting on. To me and Mum it was just a face-saving exercise in concern. She gave me half a crown, and I saw Mum's face inwardly angry and contemptible of this piece of hypocrisy. I believe that she was relieved that the damage wasn't more than it was, and Mum wasn't going to let her use us as a training ground for her do-gooding activities.

The Scotstown Moor camp gave some of us an opportunity to spend a fortnight in the country, and I enjoyed two holidays there, and was looked after by kind, hardworking staff, whose patience must have been sorely tried with our primitive practices. Pearson's Picnic, too, wasn't one of those charitable hand-outs which were doled out as a sop to the working classes. It didn't feel as if we had been placed between the horsefloat shafts of misfortune, although at nine years of age, I sometimes felt the effects of the continual ups and downs of life, and the tempting things that you saw in the shop windows and can't afford.

To me, the other side of the coin of life were the well-dressed children, looking as smug as tailors' dummies, with the money in their well-pressed pockets that never comes your way. My penny bank always seemed to be robbed when it reached the florin mark. In the classroom you always had to bid in order to get the discarded school books they hand down for your benefit. I used to hate this form of patronising, when in full view of the class I handed over my coppers for the well-used books. This act of do-gooding on their part made me even more aware of belonging in the bottom drawer of the community. Nevertheless, these long-ago teachers did a magnificent job with the material that they had; they accomplished so much with a special brand of kindness and understanding that we needed all the time in which we attended school.

Mum was obviously affected by Georgina's death, although she tried to hide her loss. I remember one evening, after I had finished my history homework, she took me on her knees and gave me a big hug. It affected me in such a way that I felt as one with her, and her sorrow. I mind snuggling up to her and saying with all my heart, "I hope that you live a million years."

Life went on at a sluggish pace; nothing seemed to go in a free way. At school, there were the usual petty quarrels amongst us. Violence would break out, and some of us would get hurt. I seemed to get more involved with library books that carried me into different worlds of thought. I was becoming more mentally allergic to the many situations that we took for granted in our daily lives, and questioned their values and truths. It has been a continuing way of probing for the very reason "why", and "why" it should be.

One day in May, a week or two short of my tenth birthday, a significant event occurred which was to be a landmark in my life. It started like most days, preparing and going to school; it was the usual dash to get there on time. When I arrived in my classroom to commence my lessons, I was somewhat lethargic in my interest to pay full attention. Later on, in the playground, the zest to play and mix with my pals had evaporated. I just felt depressed in a way that I couldn't explain. A pal of mine, George Stark, accompanied me most of the way homeward, and we parted company at Woolman-hill. When I got home to our rooms in St. Andrew Street, I opened the door and there was no Mum waiting for me. I assumed that she must be doing cleaning work and would be back shortly to make the supper. I ambled downstairs again and out on to the street. Upon spotting me, a young boy came over and said that Mum wouldn't be home, because she was dead. I just couldn't believe him; how could he know such a thing, and assumed that he was merely blethering, so drove it from my mind, but as I was walking over to the corner shop at Charlotte Street, this nagging doubt which had been in the back of my mind all day that something was wrong began to pop up again. What that young boy had told me was beginning to make me feel scared and panicky, so that I became really upset. Whilst I was leaning against the shop window, I saw Dad coming down the street to meet me, and then at once I knew that I had been told the truth. Mum dead, how could that happen; surely not my Mum? I thought that it was the end of everything, but Dad took me in his strong arms to comfort me, even though he was the loser too. He took me upstairs to the house, giving me more comfort, and together we waited for Jeannie and Edward to come home and break the awful news to them. When they appeared, it was heartbreaking for us all. As I cried my eyes out, I felt like a ship torn away from its anchor; left at the mercy of unknown elements. We went to our beds with numb minds and "sair herts". The next day also brought trouble, for Jeannie and Edward refused to go back with Dad to Short Loanings. They felt resentful towards him because he had left Mum to bring us up on her own, whilst he stayed with his mother. They were adamant that they would stay in this, their home, and fend for themselves, including me. Later on in the day, Dad took me down to Shoe Lane, where there were double doors leading into Marischal College and the University mortuary. Although his services were only required part time, the mortician lived in a cottage nearby, and had been able to attend promptly to laying out Mum's mortal remains, so when Dad lifted me up, I was able to look into the still beautiful serene face of Mum, forever etched upon my mind. Here lay Mum, a mother that any lad could be proud of; her love encompassed those brief years that we had enjoyed her loving personality. No more would she be enslaved with the hard, menial tasks that undermined her body and soul for the little reward that had kept her and her family barely existing. Did not Jesus Christ speak about "the glory of the conquered"? The bauble of "reputation" seems insignificant when set alongside her significance in the human scale of things.

Dad told me that our Mum had a heart attack whilst doing a wash for a family whom he thought were more well-to-do, that bade just off The Guestrow. They paid her the princely sum of half a crown a wash. It seemed to me to be a trifling sum, but even that could not replace a loving Mum: we had become a family of "orphans" due to the work being too heavy and sapping her strength finally. The poor always pay "the going rate" to the Ferryman.

Edward had now got a job at Broadfords, Maberly Street; Jeannie stayed at home running the household whilst I attended school, but it was apparent that this arrangement couldn't last, so Dad, with the consent of his mother, took us to their home to stay. The meagre possessions had to be carted to Short Loanings; and there was back rent to pay, and if you cannot pay, there is only one way out, and that is a "Meenlicht flitting". Dad arranged that with an old cronie who had a hand cairtie. It was around 7 p.m. that a middle-aged man presented himself with the old ricketty hurley; the two wheels were out of alignment, and the shafts were pitted with holes, just like chicken pox. As for our "porter", I thought that he looked rather pathetic. He was nearly six foot and bearded like The Bard. His face was thin and sallow; nose on the bulbous side. His clothes were rough and worn. I took him into the house and dismantled our two beds. He lightened the weight of the ogee chest by taking out the drawer, then, with the aid of ropes, guided our furniture to the street. It was "gye roch going", and not without some harsh words and knocks. It beats me how that cairtie carried such a load with the wheels out of plumb, but John had every confidence that we would see Short Loanings. As we made our way somewhat erratically down St. Andrew Street, pinpricks of light showing on the offside carriage lamp, Edward and myself also gave a push. We took the Denburn route, but had to rest at Jack's Brae in order to gather sufficient strength to overcome its steepness. A number of boys who attended Skene Street School were playing there, and gathered around the hurley, poking and looking at our worldly wealth. Surprisingly, John got them together and promptly preached to them, using stories and parables from The Bible. This turn of events certainly floored me, but after we had finished, we had numerous helpers that soon got us to the top of Jack's Brae; bore us along Leadside Road, then up to Number 27 Short Loanings, our new home. Dad came to the door and thanked John. They carried in the ogee chest of drawers, but apparently Dad had not much room for anything else, and with great generosity, he told John to keep the rest of the furniture. John accepted gratefully, for he collected odds and ends and sold them at a profit. I certainly hoped that John would make a few bob out of it. After all, he had done a great job, and a labourer is worthy of his hire. Such was my introduction to Short Loanings and my Grannie Duncan, who appeared rather strict, fussy and abrupt; but I learned in the near future that she had a great capacity for love and understanding. In leaving St. Andrew Street and Minister Lane, a lot of primitive conditions, which had been so endemic in our early lives, were left behind. Slop pails, dampness and bugs of Aberdeen awa; it was nevertheless a wary and excitable boy that approached the first night with his Dad and Granny. At least, the first thing that I noticed was the sink, and its brass-shaped water pipe fixed in a black iron cast sink, and a wooden cover that could fold down and make a platform for holding flower pots. What gave me most pleasure was a wire basket filled with flowers that had long trailing tendrils, the aspidistra and plant pots on the sink top were a revelation to me. Granny Duncan, their proud tender, was a fragile old lady whose movements were somewhat restricted. Both her legs were being treated for excess water, and they were heavily bandaged. I was horrified to see that the doctor's remedy for this disability was to cut open her legs to let the excess fluid drain away, and the glimpse that I got of her legs was one mass of red scars which lined up and down her thighs to her wasted ankles. Here to me at least, was another form of surgery that was both ignorant and cruel. The pain it must have given her whilst she ran a tight ship was another insight that I had into the courage of mothers to look after their families.

That first night with Dad, I was stripped bare, and put into a zinc bath, which he filled with hot water at just the right temperature. Then he personally soaped and scrubbed me so thoroughly that every pore in my body was cleansed. The colour and density of the water had definitely changed for the worse, but after being dried and combed, this "water baby", "Tom", was offered a cup of tea, and tucked into bed; tomorrow could look after itself. This was the best night's sleep I had had for a long time; most important, I felt fine and warm.

Rules
Tak' note ivvry een in the hoose.

The front doorie as ye cam in, shut after ye, an' the back doorie as weel.

Ivvry hooseholder tak's a turn aboot laving lobby an' keepin' clane ivvry morn.

A'body hiv, tae clane lavies an, dryin'-laft windies. See that the dryin' laft windae is kept shut a' nicht.

Waking up in the morning, I found that I was in a fairly big room, with lovely flowered wallpaper on a rich green background. There was a wooden picture rail around the walls, and more surprisingly, there were two oil paintings with heavy gold gilt frames hanging by means of a picture hook and metal chain. The fireplace was tiled with flowers on a green base too. The basket for the fire itself being set in rather an attractive bowed arch, which to my eye was unusually low-slung. The fender was cast iron too. These accoutriments were a sure sign of a "lifty-up" in the world, and the floor was actually covered with lino with the same sort of pattern as the wallpaper. When I arose, I was dressed under Granny's eagle eye. When I went to put on my boots they had already been polished, and they were shining like a mirror. When I went through to the kitchen, the table was laid for breakfast. I had a chair to sit on at the table; a blue and white bowl was filled with steaming hot porridge and accompanied by a cup of creamy milk. There was a big spoon alongside the bowl, but Edward and Jeannie got a boiled egg, along with home-baked oatcake and plenty of butter on it. It pleased me a lot that we had got a welcome start, because inwardly I was missing Mum, and it hurts a lot when you know that you will never see her in this world again. There is compensation in one way however; her strength of love has been a built-in memory for a lifetime. The time had arrived to go to school. When I stepped out on to the pavement there was a stable across the street with a shoemaker's shop; a granite-built tenement abutted it. There were a few loons and quines of my own age running up the street in the opposite direction probably to Skene Square School. As I walked down The Loaning, a boy named Bill Smith, whom I already knew came out of Number 25, and was surprised to see me. We joined up forces and passed a big yard where horses were trained for racing sometime in the future. I looked through a hole in the big double door and saw a man with a long rope making a big grey horse go round in circles. I always knew him by the name of Courage; fascinating viewing. . . As we advanced down the street, we passed a small shop run by a couple; the husband was a heavily-built middle aged man, and thought he looked a bit flash. His wife was a slender, good-looking woman; younger than her husband, and she had nice fair hair. I liked the look of her face and pleasant manner. I bought a halfpenny's worth of dolly mixtures there.

I noticed yet another corporation urinal and some partially demolished buildings, then I came upon a second hand dealer's shop. The proprietor was named Dow, and he specialised in books. Next was an oatcake bakery run by the Melrose brothers, and the establishment was called "The Heatherbell". I also took note that there was a chip shop and a grocer with the name of Charles Sang above the door.

It seemed to take a long time that day to reach the bottom of Short Loanings, but when I looked back up the street of old, and not so new buildings and tenements, it again occurred to me that this was a new and even bigger step up in life. In a fashion I sensed that there was a fight and effort in front of me; something stirred within me as usual to comfort and strengthen me to weather the cruel sea of growing up. This has been an anchor for me all of my life.

Time doesn't stop, and we lads had to be in school by 9 a.m. prompt. We ran like hares along Leadside Road, passing the old police box, then it was helter skelter down Jack's Brae to the Swines Close; up the lanie like a shot, just catching the last bell, to queue up ready to go into our classrooms.

I was still in Mrs Smith's class in Room 15, and doing sufficiently well to keep in line with her teaching. In some subjects I forged ahead and consequently enjoyed a "butterlump". I was absorbed by reading books by authors such as Marryat, G. A. Henty, Fenimore Cooper, Charles Dickens, Robert Burns, Sir Walter Scott, and such boys' papers the ilk of "The Magnet" and "The Boys Own".

I also seemed to have some talent for football, and was always in demand, when we picked sides in the playground, the Hamilton Place empty ground, or at the mecca of all football enthusiasts, the Gallowgate pitches. Quite a few good soccer players who gained fame in their later life began it all here on the hard, earthy, stoney pitches in The Gallowgate. Learning and football went well in hand with me during the last phase with Mrs Smith. In a way, she, Miss Marr and Mrs Elphinstone built up my character and mental attitudes. Their influences for good must have been distributed in many unknown channels.

We had been living at Short Loanings for a few days, when Granny Duncan unlocked her beautiful upright piano to show me her old Scots airs and music sheets. I wasn't allowed to play it or touch it as she didn't want the keys stained. My eyes always envied it, and the yen to learn it was embedded in my mind. Granny's restrictions regarding the use of the piano, in fairness, also applied to my new-found cousins who visited their Granny regularly. I met Helen Rae first, and I approved of her after being in her company during an evening get-together with Dad and Gran. Helen was a nice looking girl; fair-skinned and rather outspoken, but I liked her. Soon, I met the whole family at their home in Huntly Street: my Uncle and Auntie Rae, Douglas, John, Billy, and Ann Rae. It was with Ann that I subsequently developed a bond of sympathy and respect that has endured throughout the years. I also found that I had an Uncle Hugh Duthie and Auntie Annie, my Dad's sister. They had a daughter and a son; and the son in later life made a reputation for himself in Children's Hour on BBC radio as a bothy singer.

Uncle Hugh was a dental mechanic, and his family spent a few holidays on a farm just outside Aberdeen. When I look back, the idea of spending a holiday on a farm was a great adventure. My imagination ran amok, thinking about being involved in the work of the farm: the milking of the kye, grooming and harnessing the horses; maybe getting a shottie at ploughing the fields just like taking a feeing. I mulled over endless make-believe methods of making pin money, but it would have cost Dad ten shillings for my week's holiday, and it was out of the question even though they were kind enough to invite me. My birthday and the summer holidays were coming up and after they were over, I would be attending Mr King's classes in Room 17.

Household Hints

Uses of Borax and Bi-Carbonate of Soda

1. 1 part of borax to 2 of honey or glycerine, good for sore throats and thrush.

2. 1 teaspoonful added to washing water prevents rough skin and chapped hands; also good for flushing of face.

3. To ease cold sores, pimples and sinus trouble, rub in Bi-Carbonate of Soda.

During the summer holidays, the character of Short Loanings revealed itself as a street to live in. My first contact with the folk that dwelt in the tenements was with two boys from different families on our own stair, but it was only a passing friendship and never amounted to anything. So far, I seemed to be a bit of a loner amongst them. There was one lad that I did like, Alfie England by name. His father was the chimney sweep and had the coal store across the street under a house that was reached by a forestairs. Inside, it was like some medieval dungeon, with flickering paraffin lamps that created some visibility, but it was always in semi-darkness. It was handy for us buying a pail of coal at four pennies per stone. It was a time for searching for friendship and stability within a neighbourhood that was to be my home for "mony a lang year". I met many families and their children — the Carnies, and the Adams, who dwelt in a much older house that was almost "run-down" and derelict. There were the Christies across the street. Their boy wasn't very robust and seemed to be too ill to attend his school every day. He was a quiet mannered boy, unable to join in the rough and tumble play of the street, and was a very thin-bodied loon, and looked like a walking hospital case. Young people resembling this boy were not unusual amongst the poor and unemployed in the slum-clearance areas of our city. I played the usual street games with the Cheynes and Matthiesons and accompanied them on occasions to The Victoria and Westburn Parks, yet somehow our personalities could never blend. On the home front, I was getting more used to my new surroundings and fitting in, but my sister could never agree with her Dad and Granny, and apparently a friend in the country agreed to give her a home. When Jeannie left Short Loanings it was the last time that we were together as a family. This was a tragedy and lasting heartache that has haunted me all of my life and brought many a silent tear.

As the weeks passed by, Dad, Edward and I lived together in the bedroom as a family; Granny was in the kitchen as she became more and more confined to her bed. Dad took over the cooking, washing and the general day-to-day running of the house.

Domestically it was a time when my life style changed, and I was able to participate in more home chores; being a message boy, ca'ing the mangle, doing the lobby cleaning and scrubbing; keeping the windows clean beside ca'ing my gird down to the Fish Market to get a "fry" very early in the morning. On my way home from South Market Street I was able to go into Mitchell & Muils for the "bread" left overs. This was a meeting place where past and present friends were vying with each other for the means of survival. I also had to go down to Bendelow for his fat juicy pies, or if funds stretched to it, his apple bannocks — a great family treat. Last, but equally as important, I had to go to Martins in George Street for his penny pies. All good value for hungry folk, as were morning rolls at Murdochs, Rosemount Place, at five for twopence. I have never tasted better or cheaper rolls in my lifetime.

Cold spells presented their own challenges to families who lived in the tenements; town dwellers were sufficiently remote from the countryside where ample supplies of kindling could be culled. In October 1926, there was an unusually cold spell, and there was a situation which prevented the smooth running of towns, especially from the coal pits.

"The Parish Rates"; (the Parish of St. Nicholas operated a bleak-looking Poor's Hoose in Nelson Street, not far from the rented rooms occupied by my Granda' Donaldson Rose Duncan in Hutcheon Street, 1876).

Year 1876-7.   No. 85·6

St. Nicholas Parish, Aberdeen.

Mr Donaldson Duncan

for Subjects situated 58 Hutcheon St.

RATES OF ASSESSMENT.

OWNERS,.........Poor's Rates, 7½d. per £1 Assessable Rent.
      "School Rate," 2¼d. per £1   Do.

OCCUPANTS,
  Class I.—Dwelling-Houses, Shops, Ware-houses, Poor's Rates, &c., at 7½d. per £1 Assessable Rent.
     "School Rate," at 2¼d. per £1 Do.
  Class II.—Lands & Fishings, Poor's Rates, 3¾d. per £1.
     "School Rate," 1⅛d. per £1.

We usually got a bag of coal once a week from the coalman on his round of customers; 1/6d was his price for ½ cwt. of coal, or if he had cinders then we bought them simply because they were cheaper and that was the best of reasons. I preferred the coal because it was easier lit, and better heat came from it; however, it was a quick burner. Cinders were the very opposite, they took longer to radiate sufficient heat, and they smelled. The coal shortage happened suddenly; on a Saturday afternoon there was no coalman. Word soon got around and we were faced with a panic stations challenge which demanded prompt and drastic action. First of all, we rushed to Mr England's coalstore across the street from our house to beat the panic-stricken customers who we knew would not be far behind us. On this occasion we were able to purchase a stone of coal at 4d per stone as well as a stone of cinders at 3d. These placed together in the grate, lasted quite a long time; but the cold spell persisted and it meant that our little stock-pile of fuel was running out faster than usual despite us burning highly combustible kindling matter. The outlook was going to be grim. England's coal store was cleaned out of all stocks, and I was prepared to chop up the kitchen shelves if need be, but fortunately it didn't come to that for the Gasworks advertised in the papers that they could supply a certain amount of cinders on a ration basis; two stones for 6d. I considered it really pricey, but beggars can't be choosers, for Dad and I were allergic to the cold, and it was decided that I would go down to Cotton Street on the Saturday. I got 7d from Dad; 6d for the cinders and a halfpenny tram fare to Union Terrace but had to walk the rest, and do the same when coming home. A simple enough procedure, and I left home at 7.30 a.m. I met two or three lads who were going for cinders also; they had a cairtie to handle their load. The upshot of this meeting was that we all set off together. Upon ascertaining that we had 5d spending money between us it was agreed that when we were on the homeward run we would go in past Mitchell & Muil's Castle-gate shop for "brokeners" (the left over biscuits and wafers). This was indeed something to look forward to because if you were lucky, chocolate biscuits could be on offer too.

Household Hints

Cleaning the Linoleum
Paraffin is a splendid cleanser for this. Do not wet much in cleaning; a rub with a clean cloth damp with paraffin will remove dust and often save washing. Linoleum, after washing, should be dried thoroughly and polished with furniture polish, or rubbed over with size water, and then allowed to dry. For size water, dissolve a penny packet of size in a 2 lb. jar of water. Candle ends mixed with hot turps makes a good paste floor polish.

Young, eager legs don't waste time on a cold and frosty morning, and when we went down Baker Street towards Woolmanhill we found that there were scores of boys and girls as well as grown-ups all having the same goal in mind, so we merged with them. There were cairties, prams, barrows, and all types of improvised transport, pushed or pulled by young laddies muffled up with scarves, balaclava helmets, oversized caps. Some wearing short trousers, others with long trousers. Some even were lucky enough to be kitted out with mittens, gloves and long stockings. I noticed many of them wearing the leather "tacketty beets", (parish boots with the holes in their uppers, and laced with leather thongs). Most of the grown-ups had the same odd assortment of clothing, (anything to keep out the cold). We were no different from the rest, but we were determined to get down quicker than most. Along the way down to Cotton Street, we encountered many more people of all ages pressing on, determined to be sure of their fuel ration. A lot of the Rosemount loons that I spotted were full of devilment as they capered down "The Port". At the Gasworks, there were bobbies queuing the crowds up in a good-natured manner, teasing the winding heaving mass who were shouting or gesticulating their repartees. You couldn't help but laugh along with this medieval, yet modern, army of nondescript camp followers; it wasn't a picnic to stand and wait for nearly two hours in this climate of cold blasts which were driving inland from the flurried horizons of Aberdeen Bay. We young lads could fend for ourselves by jumping about and thus keeping the circulation in our bodies working efficiently; it must have been sheer torture for the elderly and the young women who had the extra burden of looking after wee tots.

The men, who were shovelling the cinders, weighed and filled the odd bags or boxes, and worked like Trojans, and even in this cold the sweat was running down their coal-black faces. Some of the cinders were warm still and hadn't had time to cool sufficiently. It must have been about 11 a.m. when we got our bag of cinders. Once the cairtie was loaded, we made a breenge for Mitchell & Muil to spend our fivepence on the "brokeners". We got a mix-up which included chocolate biscuits, and would you believe it, a large left-over mutton pie. These items were a great start to the day, but needless to say didn't last long due to our hunger. The food tasted all the better along with the assurance that our house would be heated during the next few days.

Getting cinders from The Gas Works became the usual practice for me during the hard years of The Twenties; during those years nothing really changed and equally entrenched in my mind is the editorial of the 1921-22 pamphlet that was put out by The Evening Express and cost ½d. The reporter saw to it that High Society did get to hear about the sacrifices that were even yet being made within the "Homes fit for heroes". This was surely not the home-coming that our brave soldiers had envisaged.

The era of the free meals at Shoe Lane had ended, and with the help of parish boots, jackets and trousers I was suitably clad to face the uncertainty of attending school for another year. My new master "Kingie" was spare in build and somewhat elderly. His face was puckered. He had a moustache, but the dome of his head was bald. He had a stoop, and was troubled with bronchitis. He always seemed to be using his handkerchief. He had a nice sense of humour, and his strapping prowess never made any deep impression. He couldn't understand anybody being poor, but that one blind spot that he had didn't prevent him from being a good teacher.

The captain of the football team, Bill Clayton, was like a God to us younger boys, and I was seeking a place so that I could play for the school. Meantime I had to wait until we were all transferred to Rosemount School. Bill went on in later years to play for the Banks o' Dee F.C.; fame indeed. Another one was Reuben Bennet who played in goal, and one evening when they were playing Causeweyend School in the cup at Nelson Street pitches, the "Cassie Enners" put eight past him into the net, but Reuben probably saved as many again. I followed his career as a professional from the time he played for Hull City F.C., then Dundee F.C.; but his greatest club was Liverpool F.C. where he remained for many years as assistant trainer.

Household Hints

CLEANING

Slimy sponges should be soaked in vinegar before washing, or washed in water with a teaspoonful of borax in it. Wooden skewers which come in joints of meat should be washed and saved for cleansing jars.

Cleaning Glass: Egg shells crushed fine in a bottle filled with cold water and well shaken will clean and brighten the glass. Ammonia is an alternative. A pinch of borax added to the washing water removes marks.

Cleaning Paint: ½ lb. yellow soap, 1 oz. borax, ½ lb. whiting, 3 pints water. Shred down the soap, put in an old pan or tin; add borax and water. Allow to dissolve over the fire, add the whiting and mix. Bottle, cork well, and use as required, rubbing on with a flannel cloth, rinsing with warm water and rub dry with a soft duster.

While I was enjoying myself, hoping to be a member of the team, something happened to change my life more acutely. It was a grey cloudy day of drizzling rain when I awoke at ten o'clock and Dad was making the breakfast. I noticed that the curtains of the bed recess were drawn, and at this time I did not know how ill Granny was. After everything was cleaned up and ship-shape, I went over to Granny's bed to see if she required anything for her comfort. I noticed that the frail old woman with sunken cheeks was breathing slowly and labriously. Her eyes were closed, not giving the slightest movement that she was conscious. I thought that I would leave her alone for a little while, and as I was about to close the curtains I heard a deep sort of sigh, and then there was complete silence. I didn't realise at that moment what had happened, but I must have taken second thoughts and leaned over her face; all breathing had stopped, and it came to me like a flash that Granny was dead. I was momentarily stunned at this happening, for it was the first time in my life that I had witnessed a life pass away in death. It took all my time to comfort Dad and how I managed to do this, time has erased from my memory. Dad took over the task of sorting things out, and in a little time, I had to go out into the rain-soaked streets and run as fast as I could to his sister Mrs Rae in Huntly Street. Knocking at her door was an emotional experience, and when the door was opened for me to enter the house, I babbled out a rush of words as to what happened. When I was a bit calmer and explained lucidly, Auntie Rae put on her hat and coat, and we hurried back to Short Loanings. This day was one of the few really black days of my life; I hadn't known Granny Duncan very long, but she took me into her house and looked after me when my world fell about me due to the death of my loving and generous Mum. Yes, Granny Duncan, ill as she was, gave what her heart had in full: love, shelter and understanding; nobody could ask for more.

Auntie Anne from Glasgow and the rest of the family gathered to arrange the funeral; like all families in our position, duties of funeral arrangements had to reflect our love and respect for our deceased family, and that costs money. Dad and his two sisters made arrangements for the funeral, and apparently came to the decision that the piano would have to go in order to get over the money shortage. When I heard that the Scottish music as well as the piano was going I felt a pang of being cheated momentarily, but when I thought about the kindness and good will shown to me, it disappeared like a shot into limbo.

The morning dawned for the funeral; everything had been prepared for the service, and the table was laid with refreshments for the mourners who wished to pay their outgoing respects to the bereaved family.

It was arranged that Helen, Ann Rae plus myself would occupy one of the horsecabs to St. Peter's Cemetery, situated in Merkland Road, King Street. As the family mourners drove away, it soon came to our turn to go in our hansom cab, drawn by a big black horse, suitably harnessed. The cab driver was thin-faced, and wore a lum hat. He was perched on his high seat, holding a long, slender whip.

Despite the funeral occasion, I could hardly contain my excitement when I clambered inside. Then, there was a sharp crack of the whip, and we were in motion, and in another instance the horse began trotting up Short Loanings, with its steel-shod hooves beating a rhythmatic tattoo on the granite cassies of the street. Looking out, we waved to some of the people we knew, almost in a condescending fashion, but a first time ride in a hansom cab gave a feeling of regal pomp, but as we gathered speed, the passing scenes gave way to the cast-iron cemetery gates, where the undertakers were silently bearing Granny Duncan to her last house; and as we followed the coffin, the sadness of the moment forced a tear of regret for the woman who had borne what faith and fortune had doled out to her with Faith, Conviction and Courage.

The next few weeks seemed to pass quickly without any special event arising through this period of mourning. Dad had now taken over the tenancy of the house. The bits and pieces left behind by Granny were divided amongst the family.

Household Hints

Care of Boots and Shoes

To make last longer.—Boots can be made to last much longer, if, before wearing them, you oil the soles with cold-drawn linseed oil for 3 or 4 days in succession, and put them, soles upwards, to allow the oil to soak in each time. When you take off your boots, you lay them on their sides, they will wear longer.

To polish new boots.—Rub over with half a lemon and leave till thoroughly dry. Repeat once or twice if necessary.

Creaking boots can generally be cured by soaking the soles in salt water, then leaving them overnight in linseed oil. If not successful, hammer three or four sprigs through the outer sole.

At this time of flux, Dad was sometimes visited by a Jake MacDonald, who lived with his brother Willie in a rundown hovel situated on The Lang Stracht. Now and again Dad returned the compliment by visiting them, mostly in the evenings. He took me one night, and upon going up a steep, narrow flight of wooden stairs, we entered a small, dark room, faintly illuminated with a small burning oil lamp. As my eyes got accustomed to the gloom, I saw this old-looking man. He was unshaven, and his hair was sparse. He lay on a bundle of sheets, and the pillowcases had seen better days; Willie was a victim of acute arthritis and his legs were bent double. He bade me sit down on the edge of the bed in a gravelly, shaky voice. Jake told his brother that I was at school, and it delighted me to tell them that I was playing football for the school team. It seemed to make an impression on them, and I was sitting away listening to them talking when my eyes wandered across to the smokey, grimy, dingy walls, for the oil lamp was making queer fantastic shadows. When I looked up to the ceiling I got the impression that the whole surface of the ceiling had changed into a different pattern. I convinced myself that I must have been dreaming. When Dad and me finally left the brothers' company and were walking down The Lang Stracht, I thought that I would ask Dad about the phenomena that I had seen on the roof. He just looked down at me and gave a laugh and said, "You noticed it; that was the blue bottlers, they're an inch thick, and have been in possession for years."

The two brothers may have come down to this level, but they once had a big farm on Westburn Road, along with a sister. Their father was a Professor of Theology, but Jake and Willie were not cast in the same mould, and were totally unable to run their inheritance. They employed the most unsuitable persons, most of them only capable of argument, whose stock in trade was debating upon theological trivia. One of them was nick-named "The Professor of Potterton". He was a thin, ungainly man, with an unusually large head, which in anthropological terms was taken as the signs of high intelligence. "The Professor" himself however would down tools at the drop of a hat to indulge in any comment even faintly relating to theology. His appetite belied his physical appearance. Dad told me that one day, as dinner time was approaching, the sister, who laid the table for some half a dozen persons, told "The Professor" that she had to go out unexpectedly, and would he tell the others when they too stopped for lunch. "The Professor", who was feeling hungry, promptly went into the kitchen and scoffed the lot.

The others arrived to find him fast asleep. This is only one example of the kind of chaos that ensued on their farm. In due course, "The Professor" decided to flit back to Potterton, and asked Jake if he would oblige him by taking his possessions from a small room that he occupied in a tenement near the arched entry on to The Gallowgate at the top of the brae in Littlejohn Street. The two-wheeled farm cairt was pulled by a strong, heavy Clydesdale horse, and as Jake commenced to load up, a number of scavengers or loafers were standing around at the door. Jake had been under the impression that it was a load of furniture to be flitted, but when he entered the dim-lit room, he was amazed to stumble upon a huge pile of lum hats, too small for the average Aberdonian cranium; consequently they had become surplus stock at the hatter's shop, many of them green with age and dampness, amongst other eccentric items that made up the cargo. Jake was embarrassed at the cat-calls and shrill whistling as he made his way round the corner into The Gallowgate, and so out to Potterton. Jake and Willie MacDonald acted in a "Keystone Cop" manner, and my "silent movie" impressions of them continue with "The Saga of The Mutton Brae". They grew a lot of vegetables on the farm in those days and sold them at either The Castlegate or The Green. The previous day, Jake had bought a Galway Blazer, one of the Firemaster's surplus horses. It was accustomed to the sound of firebells. The MacDonalds were not very fussy about keeping their harness in trim, and they suddenly found that they were short of a leather reins. They took rather a hasty decision to use woollen reins instead. They set off from the farm, laden with country produce and were trundling down Skene Square nae bother, when the horse heard a fire engine rushing up, its bell ringing frantically en route to the scene of a fire. As it passed by, Jake's horse reared up in the air then clamped down again with a great thud, and bolted towards The Mutton Brae past Black's Buildings. Jake and Willie tried in vain to regain control, but the woollen reins had snapped, so their load was scattered all along Woolmanhill and The Mutton Brae. As the Galway Blazer entered The Green, it was miraculously halted in its tracks, as suddenly as it had bolted, which gave a coup de grace to the cart and contents. Some of the less well-off citizens enjoyed vegetable soup for nearly a week, gratis. Jake consoled himself, as was his wont, with iced fruitcakes from Murdoch the baker in Rosemount Place. He usually bought half a dozen and had eaten maybe two before he reached "The Cocket Hat", a field at the beginning of The Lang Stracht. He rested here to fill in his Strang's football coupon, and munch another of his fruitcakes. On one occasion he hit the jackpot, £600. After the excitement of this big win, he thought that he might like a holiday in the town; he asked our help and we got him into The Northern Hotel, which was then an old fashioned privately run establishment. Mrs Cooper had her doubts about his appearance, nevertheless his creditworthiness won the day. He had been four days in the hotel when I decided to run down to see how he was getting on. As I entered the hallway I heard the shrill voice of a woman giving somebody a dressing down. It was Jake in trouble, and upon seeing me Mrs Cooper grabbed me and propelled me into Jake's bedroom to see what he had done. His brown tobacco juice had stained the wall very noticeably, and we both got the heave-ho from the hotel. Jake couldn't understand the mess or fuss he had created. It was a habit that came naturally to him. Not long after that, Jake and Willie were put into The Oldmill Hospital where they lingered for a while until they died because they gave up hope living in an institution. Today in The Lang Stracht it is as if the life and times of the brothers MacDonald had never been; their connection with the place completely severed. There was another erudite character that I used to visit at "The Aulmill"; his name was William Martin. He originally came from Esslemont Avenue. He was a helpless, all thumbs individual, but he had a great theological knowledge, and when he came and saw us on his daily round of the city I learned a lot about the Old and New Testament and their meanings from him. William was the messenger who delivered the hospital mail, and he got money for his tram fares which he never put to use, having it for twenty years. He must have saved over £200, but no fairy tale ending for him, he was found dead in one of the W.C.'s during the forenoon. William's savings went back to the hospital, where he got them in the first place; such was the rigidity of the system. Hardship and restricted opportunity can sometimes lay the foundation and be the pattern of thoughts being fertilised and convictions of spiritual aspirations. This may well have been the most fallow, fortunate phase of my life meeting this older company; pals of my father's and gaining significant insight into human nature through Dad being a doyen of their foibles, which seem innocent enough in today's society.

Household Hints

Cleaning Ornaments

Brass benefits with an application of ammonia, turpentine and paraffin. Steel ornaments can be cleaned with vinegar.

The time was now approaching when my time at Skene Street School would be at an end, for the Control Exams were a hurdle that had to be crossed, and we were all on edge about the transfer to Rosemount School and what would happen to us there. The tempo began to accelerate in the classroom. What we previously had done was rigorously gone over and revised; then before we realised it, we were all seated at our desks, going through the exam papers, and plying our minds to answer the questions. The papers were then scooped up, and in my case the gates of Rosemount School were opened up.

I walked up the way with Bill Smith, who lived at 25 Short Loanings. We didn't speak about school, but commented about a large telescope that was being built in California, the biggest in the world, and it would be ready in two years' time; such are young boys' minds. I had given my trophies to Dad, who put them away in the ogee chest, to lie mostly unnoticed for a lifetime. Looking down this time tunnel I see how he appreciated my efforts. The Good Lord speaks about "the Glory of the conquered". School reports deserve a place alongside the Family Bible in that old-fashioned kist of wordly goods.

During the first week or two of the holidays, I tried to mix with the other lads in the top half of The Loanings, but it wasn't a complete success, but I did get along with Dod Hepburn, and the Rudd brothers who lived in Magdala Place, a small street off Short Loanings with a row of decent tenement houses, but I never did get a chance to squinter through them. Coulter's Dairy had their stable at the back of the tenements. There was always something going on most of the day with the early morning bustle of the carts and cairters delivering their milk to their awakening customers. After all, porridge and tea are better with milk. Magdala Place had the distinction of having a church, St. Marks, (Episcopalian) at the corner of the street and Short Loanings. It was of wood and corrugated metal construction, but it served its worshippers very well. The enclosed space at the door of the church was a popular meeting place for young people. I spent many a happy hour there playing "chuckies", consisting of five small stones; a game of picking up or putting down these chuckies, and another popular game called "droppies". This was a game where you slapped a cigarette card against the wall, to flutter down and touch any other cigarette card lying on the ground. I bought my cigarette cards from Dow's shop, where I also got my comics. It was here that I met Johnnie Dow, and his brothers Jim and Bill. They enjoy a reputation for being a nice, obliging family.

On the corner of Leadside Road was a tenement known as "The Tower", a Scottish Baronial pile in appearance. It was occupied by numerous families. Sang the grocer had his shop here, ably assisted by Charlie Lindsay. Their kindness to me all the years that I lived in The Loanings has never been devalued at any time. Another kindly man was Mr Cheyne, who delivered his newspapers on a big bike. I, myself, delivered A. B. Hutchison's morning rolls six mornings in the week for the princely sum of two shillings. In some tenements, the smell of floor polish struck you, for the lino in the lobby was highly polished. There was even lino on the stair treads and carpets on the landings, and I used to think that it was marvellous that they weren't stolen. This was a contrast to the small dilapidated tenement next to "The Tower" where I met Billy Reid, a very athletic boy who played a smashing game of football. Billy played for Skene Street School and Rosemount School. Later he played for the East End Junior Club at Advocate's Park, then he was signed up by Aberdeen F.C. Not bad for a Leadside Loon.

In its way, the empty space of ground at the foot of The Loanings was a happy playing ground for us, where "the bools" were the top interest. The ground had "kypies" dug all over the place, with a dozen games going on at the same time. This was the era of the "clay doddie", "pick", "glassers", "steelies"; also "knuckling" experts, and "the dead shot" experts. They helped to make the champion, and of course a huge collection of marbles. It gave you status amongst the less successful. Further up Short Loanings was a large empty space with one or two derelict buildings. On most afternoons, more so Saturdays, the bookies runners had their stance there. Some of them had their newspapers on the walls with all the race meetings displayed. Bookies and betting were regarded as unsocial, but for them who had to exist on a very small income they were a life saver; many a luxury or a rent being paid with the success of a tanner double. Saturday night around 6 p.m. was the settling hour, and if you had a "shottie" up on the horses, you were paid out. Many a punter had Saturdays at 6 p.m. for a reason to celebrate. If you picked your horses right, and the odds were right, a "gie few quid" for a 3d or 6d bet was something. It may have paid your Saturday night out, and the expenses for the following week. The Runner had his troubles, seeing that it was against the law; by tacit agreement with the "bobbie" on the beat, he was charged with unlawful betting every two months. Usually a fine of £1, or ten shillings. Justice was

seen to be done. Yes, the bookies runner was a popular and respected part of the neighbourhood. They survived because they were honest. Another form of betting was the "fixed odds" coupon. I still mind on the popular "Jamieson" coupon, another source of income for some lucky people. It was not impossible for some professional people, who tried to manipulate the results to their advantage.

The morning delivery job gave me a chance to visit places like the cinema or get a shilling bag of fruit or chocolate, or the chance to see a picture, variety or stage drama at H.M. Theatre; usually a seat in the "Gods" for fourpence. I remember going to see "Pearl White", also Maria Martin or "The Red Barn". Harry Lauder, along with his twisted walking stick, and at "The New Kinema" in Belmont Street I first saw that old western silent classic "Covered Waggons". The "'Lechies" in Union Street I visited once or twice, also "La Scala", the interior of which was pitch black. You used to stumble to your seat. There wasn't much help from the ushers. "The Picture House" was the prestigious cinema. The staff were all spit and polish, there were tip-up seats and a marvellous screen for film viewing. Incidentally, it was where I first heard Martin Downey the Irish tenor. The other cinemas like "The Star", and "The Casino", were houses of mayhem, especially on a Saturday afternoon. "The Flechie Kings" cinema in George Street was popular, and they never failed to give an apple or orange free at Christmas. Sometimes you could "swick" one. I think that the doorman had a heart of gold.

Household Hints

Cleaning the Furniture

A good and cheap polish is made from equal quantities of turpentine and raw linseed oil. Half these quantities each of methylated spirits and vinegar. Measure into a clean bottle and shake well. Keep tightly corked and shake before using. For light woods and mahogany, a cream is necessary. 1 oz. beeswax, ½ oz. white wax, ½ oz. soap, ½ pint of turpentine, ¼ pint water. Shred down the waxes, place in a clean jam jar and cover with the turpentine. Dissolve the soap in the water, add to the turpentine. Stand by the fire until the wax is dissolved.

White marks on polished wood can be removed with spirits of camphor.

Leather furniture can be cleaned by washing the dirt with water, using a flannel, rinse with a clean flannel and water and dry thoroughly. Polish with furniture polish, or slightly beaten white of egg. Another way:— Mix 1 part vinegar with two parts linseed oil and polish well.

Cane bottomed chairs or rush chairs should be first well brushed and sprinkled with salt water and set in the open air to dry. Wicker chairs benefit by an application of paraffin. Dirty chair covers should be rubbed with hot bran to clean.

I often went to the parks on my own and made a few friends; especially the cricketers, and although I got a few knocks, it was great fun playing with them. I developed a good scoring bat, and my bowling prowess snaffled a few wickets. Dad encouraged me to mix, but with the right ones. There was no letting up with my duties at the house; they had to be done. Dad in exchange "soutered" my football boots if they required it, also my everyday walking boots. He had a box of tools for the purpose: knife, rosetty twine, blackening ink and wax, an iron for melting the wax on the edges of the shoe. He had an "iron devil" for the shoe to lie onto; cut and shape the leather. This he bought from Hyland the leather merchant, Broad Street. To make a good repair with it you had to soak it, then hammer it for it was non-porrous, then it was stitched with "Tingles", small, headless tacks; fit it and solder with wax after giving it a file with the rasp, and give the wax a smooth over, pare the leather to balance with the rest of the sole then paint it over with blackening ink. Dad usually put a stud round the edge of the shoe to walk properly and keep up your balance with the other foot.

In the last few days of our holidays, I went with Dad and a friend of his to pick "blaeberries" at Kingswells. What a slow, patient, back-breaking job it is; we had a "piece" to sustain us, and continued working until our baskets were full, and we made tracks for home. Dad carried me on his shoulders for three miles but help was at hand, for a steam-driven coal lorry stopped and gave us a lift to King's Gate. When we came down the road to Short Loanings, we weighed our "blaeberries" and found that we had gathered 16 lbs. apiece, which meant jam tomorrow and a few morrows after that, but I never get tired of eating "blaeberry" jam pieces. The last day of freedom was a time of preparation: clothes made tidy and clean; this was a combined operation for Dad and I. It made me quite an expert at threading a needle and how to use it. I got out the zinc bath and filled it with hot water, along with a sponge, cloth and "Kiltie" soap. After I had been scrubbed and towelled dry, Dad got out the scissors for a short back and sides haircut. I was properly prepared for any eventuality or spot check examination to prove otherwise. On that sunny Monday morning, I crept up towards my new school "Rosemount", my imagination working overtime between fear and hope. It wasn't a very enthusiastic young pupil who turned the corner into Rosemount Place, passing the Co-op grocer, butcher and hardware shops; just up a few strides was the fruit and sweetie shop kept by two sisters, then straight up to Esslemont Avenue,

passing a grocer's shop which was run by a couthy, sharp-witted man. At the other side of the street was a huge, impressive building of granite with a big entrance door, that led to a flight of stairs and a hall where we were all to assemble. I saw the headmaster in conference with his teachers sorting out all the problems and snags. In no time, the lads with whom I was going to be mates with for the next two years were marched into Room 6 to face what was in store for us. When we were all seated at our desks, a tall, handsome man of about thirty-five years of age came in and sat at his desk. We knew then that "School" had begun. He gave us a slow penetrating look that made us uneasy. He must have been wondering what he was going to make of this motley crew, but after a few minutes he stood up and introduced himself as Mr John Maclean, our English teacher, and principal master. He then proceeded to make up his class register, and with the names called, there were a few of my pals from Skene Street School, Rossie Hunter, also Bobby Stevenson. Alec Crockett from Mile End School was included too.

Going from class to class, it has occurred to me that there must be some sort of freemasonry amongst the teaching staff; they all give the same advice . . . "good behaviour", "pay attention to the board", "work hard", "no sliding with homework", "best handwriting", "failure to observe any of these conditions could be the reluctant use of the strap"; past experience told me that this was excellent advice, but two or three of the class learnt the hard way. The first task was to write out a lesson prospectus for the week, with the teacher's name, subject and time. I looked at the maths column to find out the teacher's name, which was George Dickie. Well, as time went on I had the lot, and my summing up of these teachers is: Mr John Maclean was an excellent teacher of English; vain, yet fair, and could use the strap with effect. George Dickie, maths master, likeable and efficient. His aim with pieces of chalk could be very accurate, so that pupils would be jolted to attention. Corker Ross, World War victim with a leg blown off, taught us poetry appreciation. His job was hard going; no wonder he called us fat, lazy lumps of human flesh. I still think that he did a good job to give us some culture. Miss Bennett, the French teacher, was called "Dainty Dinah". She must have had some success with us because I can still speak "pidgin" French. She later married a science teacher, but we gave her respect. I learned a lot about "loyalty", especially the loyalty that schoolboys believe that is a sacred vow; but as regards myself, I condemned one side of it and silently confess for another side of "Loyalty"; a deep, lasting admiration and respect for it.

Two or three of my pals, not because they were backward, lacked interest or conviction to adjust themselves to classroom lessons and plan for the future. They, in a way, thought that it was sloppy and posh to pursue such things. As regards myself, I liked school and worked at my exams and homework. The result was that I sat in the top division, whilst my mates were in the first or second division; therein lay my problem. My school friends began to deride my place in the class, and thought that I was coming the "Tin" man. If we were to be pals, why not sit together? Well, at first, I swallowed this brand of "Loyalty", and cheated myself by neglecting classroom work and failing to do proper preparation at home. The way of doing things nearly came home to roost with my rapidly declining place in the classroom. I nearly landed in the two lower divisions at this stage, and Mr Maclean got stuck into me for lack of attention and poor performance. This was the crunch, and I knew that I was going to be the victim of his strap, which made me drastically revalue my loyalty to my friends. The answer was that it was not on. It was sheer folly to uphold such a childish code of honour. I knew that I was on the right track when the results of a special essay about the Aberdeen Beach undertaken by the whole class were made known, by Mr Maclean. He walked to the top of the class holding a sheaf of essay papers; the way he paused, and passed his lynxean eye slowly over the classroom as if debating with himself what he would say. Then, in a quiet voice he said that it hadn't been too bad for us crowd. Then he slightly turned his head and looked at me saying "Duncan, your paper was easily the best; I am glad that you are beginning now to know that education can be a good thing"; and from that time I pursued what I had to do.

The other lesson that I learnt about loyalty was an occasion when three boys in the class decided to run away to London for fame and fortune. With hindsight, it seems a hare-brained idea, but with the imagination and exuberance of young minds, it was on a par with the exploits of the great explorers of history. Their adventure came to a dead stop when they reached Stonehaven. It was like a Roman Triumph when the three heroes turned up at school the next day. Behind the scenes, Authority was planning a short, sharp, painful retribution for their audacious behaviour. A day or two

afterwards, we were in the science room, and were sticking in at our experiments, when the door suddenly opened and in came two teachers. In particular it was Mr Maclean whose face looked grim and taut. He was holding a big black strap in his hand. The runaways, namely Bill McDonald, George Mclaren and Bobby Stevenson were called out to the front of the class; arrayed in front of the teachers and their crimes read out. The punishment was six of the best, three on each hand. These three lads never said a word and shared the blame equally. Then John unrolled the strap for action; he raised their hands by the finger tips, then the punishment began on each of both hands. The strap came down on their palms just like bombs exploding. The horror of their pain, coupled with their stoic fortitude, compelled me to admire their loyalty for one another. When I remember this strict method of punishment, the cold shivers of pain engulf me; that was a loyalty of rare quality.

The Gallowgate became more familiar to me as my Rosemount School days were drawing to an end. Father had a cousin who had two outfitters shops in The Gallowgate; one on the corner of Gerrard Street and Gallowgate, and the other one further up near the United Free Church.

The name of Peter McGregor & Co. was going to be well known in the future with my periodic visits to the shops, for the time came when his open-handed generosity clothed me and suitably shod me, to make me respectable and smart, socially. Dad and I have much to thank Mr Gow for; during those difficult years which face a youth, as he makes the demanding transition from a schoolboy without a mother to see the niceties of life for him. His benevolence made the difference.

Many a time, I wended, or sped up Hutcheon Street, or that dark, tenemented, narrow Gerrard Street to his shoe and clothing shop. If I had a spare copper or two, I headed for Greigie's sweetie shop for a bag of smush, or if fancy took me, two fondant mice, (a halfpenny each).

The Gallowgate wasn't a pretty sight at any time; just a conglomoration of decaying buildings, with one or two in better condition, standing isolated amidst its old aged companions; but the local people were far from feeble: They were gutsy, kindly and hard-working — very much aware of their environment. They fought with determination to refute the nasty and ill-deserved reputation which they were saddled with. There was no shadow of doubt that the majority of families had to contend and live with the most elementary of hygiene facilities, and it says a lot for their courage that they put such a cheerful face upon their adversities. The Gallowgate, despite its unsought for reputation, has given Aberdeen many worthy citizens and patriots. Dad used to speak about some of the old courts off The Gallowgate, namely Paterson's Court, Findlay's Court and Porthill Close, with tenements that were badly overcrowded and "primitive", as he put it. Most of them had had open drains in his youth, which made them the breeding grounds of typhus and "The White Scourge". Dad said that "hell" couldn't have been worse than this earthly cesspool with its scrofulant sores." It surprised me to hear that the Police authorities had been responsible for this human morass at one time. I couldn't believe that an established local authority with all its pretensions of civilised government had overlooked these demeaning conditions which they expected other human beings like them, "God's children", to live in. I believe that the Salvation Army did however try, but not always with success, to alleviate these people's miseries. It was too expensive, it seemed, for the Local Bureaucrats to improve their lot; it was much cheaper to forget . . . after all, in conditions such as these, life expectancy was a matter of chance.

The Gallowgate, despite its gloom and shortcomings had a great attraction for many a young schoolboy who thought that they were cast in the mould of old time stars such as Alex Morton, Big Bob McPhail, Jock Hutton and Alex Jackson. All roads led up to The Gallowgate pitches next to The Middle School. Many old buildings were demolished to make way for a site to house the Royal Marquee for the King's courtiers' use when Marischal College was opened in 1906. This was the mecca, or battleground, where hundreds of enthusiastic young boys sweated, toiled, spat blood and often collected serious bruising just to be like their heroes. Most of the East End schoolboys played here which led to a friendly rivalry amongst them, with many having nicknames like "ba heid", "square heid", "pirn taes", "Ram" or "jinky", and others too unmentionable to name. The Gallowgate pitches were two large pieces of rough, stoney-earthy ground that split them in two segments, stretching from The Gallowgate to Seamount Place. Somewhere, often in far-flung places, there is yet to be found East End Aiberdeen loons, many who may have made their mark in the soccer game, and will look back at his humble beginnings with nostalgic thought or memory to replay those golden moments all over again.

The Middle School (closed 1975) had a swimming pool which was open for tuition to all pupils from local schools. Too many learnt the hard way by not acquiring swimming skills, so consequently were involved in drowning tragedies.

I had the good fortune, when I was a teenage boy, to have some contact and relationship with Bob Cooney. He lived in, or around The Gallowgate; it could have been Berry Street, which was just another impoverished area running from Loch Street to The Gallowgate; made only more resepectable at a later date, (1936), by a block of "Viennese" style tenements, (the year before Bob volunteered to help out the cause of the Spanish Civil War).

My first impressions of Bob Cooney was his forthright, challenging method in discussing local problems, and why they were problems to them; not by choice, but by design. Much of it was beyond the minds of his listeners. he spoke of Privilege, Property, Profit, Mansions and Middens. His answers to all this was Revolution by the downtrodden, to bring Justice and Wealth to be used collectively to create a Socialist Society for the betterment of The People. As a young lad, I believe that Bob Cooney absorbed the inequality in our tier-divided fabric of national reward; its tyranny and subjection of working people to a level of poverty and slavery only in order to sustain a way of life that demanded its very existence. He became a convert to the political pursuit of Communism; that was his decision, and I believe he wore that philisophy with dignity, honour and honesty. A rare quality of truth to attain in whatever generation of the city's history. Many an enjoyable debate I had with Bob concerning his militant outlook, but I sincerely believe that universal compassion, as preached by Jesus Christ, was sufficient, without recourse to violence. Rabbie Burns interpreted these teachings with the power of his poetry, amply illustrating the truth and power of the Messianic promise. "It shall come, for a' that, an' a' that". Whatever the opinions of city snob or noveau riche, The Gallowgate was a very useful and important lesson for me to learn. It gave life and strength to others like me within the body of Aberdeen. Without it, I would have been less of an individual, and an Aberdonian.

Time went on with its usual placidity at school, until the last days of our schooling drew nigh. Fears for the future, hopes and ambitions being the subject of discussion amongst us. The day came when we were massed together as a class, then the harsh clang of the bell told us that it was time to disperse and go our separate ways. As I wound my way homewards at snail's pace, full of emotion at the parting, I stopped for a few minutes at the grocer's shop at the top of The Loanings, and the full measure of the parting from school flooded into my mind. I panicked a little, but a comforting feeling reassured me that tomorrow was another day and it would solve its own problems. I took confidence with that frame of thought and walked with certain footsteps home, then closed the door to all that.

After tea time, Dad spoke to me about how I felt about leaving school, and what I had in mind as a career. I spoke of getting an apprenticeship to a trade, but Dad remarked that it would be rather difficult to find one. He drew upon his own experience as a school leaver. The most important task at the moment was to get "a blind alley job", and make enquiries, as well as write to the various shops.

Later, during the following week, I received a letter asking me to come down to the Employment Department for school leavers at Union Terrace. When the important day arrived, I was suitably attired as I went up the stone staircase into a grandeur that I had never encountered before. There was a man in uniform who directed me to the waiting room, in which two or three boys were sitting on chairs waiting their turn for an interview. They were silent, and probably scared stiff. I was rather curious what lay behind that closed door myself. I suppose that it may have been an hour, or longer, when that mystery door opened, and I was asked to come in and see a man, who was sitting behind a desk, with a lot of boxes and book files heaped in front of him. He looked through his rimless spectacles at me, pursed his lips, then asked me my name, age and address. What transpired then must have been a carbon copy of what he had performed a hundred times in the past. He picked up a few green cards, looked at me for one minute or two and said that there was only one vacancy at the moment, and if I wanted it, I would probably get it. He added that it was for the Blind Asylum in Huntly Street; no information about the job. I would find out when I got there. I duly arrived at their office and was shown through to a Mr Balfour, who sent me through to the warehouse foreman to find out what my job involved, and what was expected of me. I didn't concentrate on "the pey";

and conditions of service, I was thinking how I could help these blind people. I stood there like the shining morning-faced schoolboy as I stood to attention. The foreman was a tall, sallow-faced man; thin, with brushed-back black hair. He wore spectacles, and his official uniform seemed to be a grey coat. After inspection and interrogation, he told me to follow him, and we then went along a small passage which entered a well-stocked room of brushes, mops, mats, cane baskets, etc. This room, I had to keep tidy; in addition, go messages, deliver parcels and guide one of the blind travellers around the town. I hadn't been but half an hour on the job, when a young fellow came and saw me. He said that his name was Ian Smith, and that his uncle, Mr Balfour, was manager of the place, so relations were firmly established. During the first week, I tidied up the room and the errands took me all around the city; walking all the way, and if it took till after 5.45 p.m., then that was your hard luck. Two or three days of the week, I guided this blind traveller around the city for orders. He was elderly, and inclined to be a bit heavy around the jowls; nevertheless, his face was red-cheeked, but despite his seemingly jovial appearance, he could be a bit irascible on occasions. Then it was a chauve being with him. I had to do frequent internal department messages, and often saw blind men or women, usually elderly, sitting on a blanket on top of a wooden platform, working away making basket work. I felt very sorry for them; their working conditions were just open sheds, rather tatty; in fact, the whole set-up shouted workhouse gloom. There didn't seem much fight amongst them. I suppose that some people might say that they were lucky having a job, but I had different thoughts . . . I had been there a few weeks, and when in the stock room, Ian was usually in my company. He liked nothing better than a rumble up, until "The Big Man" came unexpectedly on the scene, and we were ordered to stand to attention, and I was issued orders to report to H.Q. Ian wasn't on the charge sheet, but it didn't really matter because I liked him even though my name was deleted from the wage sheet. It was a Godsend to go away from these surroundings.

I got full support from Dad; it was always his inclination to get a job for me in which I would acquire an interest and be happy to work at; accompanied by a practical salary. Being chopped by the "B.A." (Blind Asylum) was a blessing in disguise. It opened up for me the prospects of a new job; the job of delivering milk in the West End with Mr Peters of The Albert Dairy. Little did I think that the job was a crossroads which would affect my working life and outlook.

Starting a job at 5 a.m. needs willpower and enthusiasm: especially if its rising from a warm bed and putting your feet on to the ice-cold lino; you don't waste any time dressing and getting the kettle boiling for a cuppie of tea; then comes the prospect of opening the front door and stepping into a drab, dark morning with a Scotch mist-rain whipped up by a strong wind. It is advisable to wear a coat of any kind. The familiar silhouettes of tenements seemed to merge with one another. The street lamp, still dimly-lit, shedding an eerie, spluttering light through the arc of which I made a frightened dash down the street past "The Tower", (a massive Baronial-style tenement), into Leadside Road; scarcely noticing the glimmer of light in the recesses of Sang's grocery shop, or the more visible signs of the early-rising Mr Cheyne. I gathered speed as I crossed the junction of Esslemont Avenue and onward to Whitehall Place, on the Grammar School side; passing by this ancient stronghold of Learning; knowing what it represented, a symbol of Patronage and entrenched Privilege, which only bestowed its "favours" on one section of the community who bought, sold or determined the very existence and living standards of the majority of their fellow citizens. Yes, indeed, they supped the double cream of education; we got skimmed milk and made the best of it. When I was attending Skene Street School, the only portion of The Grammar School that I had seen, happened to be the football pitch which we were allowed to use; the rest was under lock and key. I assumed that "The Scruff" or "The Primitives" could not be allowed to pollute these hallowed halls of "Tradition"; yet my mind knew the convoluted turns that lay within that maze — it held no mysteries for me. All those thoughts which came crowding in, served to hasten my steps in order to reach Albert Dairy at least ten minutes before getting "yoked". I felt in a better humour to face anything.

At the front door of The Albert Dairy, (52 Albert Street), stood the milk floats. One was a four wheeler, the other a two wheeler. Both required to be loaded for the morning delivery. As I entered, Mr Peters was busy filling the bottles with milk, and Mrs Peters was also hard at it filling a lot of tin milk cans for delivery. Looking up at me he said, "You'll be the new laddie; we hinna muckle time jist noo, but mak' a start wi' filling these crates wi' the bottlies an' pit them on that cairt wi' the fower wheels; yer driver will be alang in a meenit or twa, an' he'll pit ye richt. See hoo quick ye can be." I just got stuck in and soon I was joined by my driver Adam Strachan who, as it happened, came from Magdala Place, just opposite our house at No. 27 Short Loanings. In no

time at all seemingly, we were loaded to start, and as I was on the point of leaving, perched on the high seat, I can even yet remember Mr Peters shouting "Be careful; I dinna wint ony broken bottles . . . they're nae cheap." Adam asked me my name, and I told him it was Davie Duncan, and he retorted "Ye seem tae be aricht, bit jist dee fat ye're telt; stick in, an' be honest, an' we'll get on fine."

As we turned into Osborne Place the morning continued to be dark and inclement. It was drizzly and caul', and this, the beginning of the West End, struck me as being a straight-laced line of terraced houses, standing on parade, and there was a military bearing about them all; "Honour" and "Loyalty" being their colonels in charge. The lamps cast bleak, glittering fingers of light upon the wet roads and pavements, and it crossed my mind that soon, I would be meeting The Middle Classes on their own territory. I was just another East End laddie opening a new door of The Toon. We completed the delivery with little bother and arrived back at the shop at about nine-thirty. Mr Peters' first words to Adam were "Weel, hoo did the laddie get on . . . didna' brak' onything . . . that's jist fine." Turning to me he said "Here is a cup o' milk an' a bap. Ye maun be hungry. Eat up, then get the cairt ready for collectin' — we're gie short o' time this morn, but dinnae rush yer piece." Mr Peters was indeed a gentleman. He was a small, elderly man with a nervous disposition. He was moustachioed and utterly respectable. His wife was a spare-figured woman whom I thought could be a real battle axe when she chose. I noticed that she was a confirmed workoholic, and somehow I felt that she was more "bark" than "bite". This was the first time that I had encountered a fierce middle class independence such as hers. (They stayed at Number 3, Osborne Place, just having their feet in the door of the West End).

Soon enough we were back on our way to where we had started, and Adam, my driver, gave me the list of doors for the special orders, (cream etc.). We had two cans of milk with taps, along with a small can for cream. We were well stocked with supplies of farm butter and eggs. Skimmed milk had to be ordered.

My first contact was with a gie auld body who "winted a pint o' milk an' a shilling of cream", and handed over a half crown along with her milk jug and a smaller one that she used for the cream. Milk was three (old) pennies, and her order came to the total sum of 1/3d. When I brought back her order and change she looked inside the jugs to see if the measure was correct then accepted her change, just saying "That seems to be aricht." There and then I decided to make it my business to be very attentive to my customers' wants and wishes, for it would make my job easier and more interesting. When we eventually turned into Blenheim Place with its more apparent grandeur and opulence, it made me wonder what manner of people made up the ambience of this street. It was Blenheim Place that gave me the new experience of being a servant of The Public. This was the "delivering goods" procedure. It was not the accepted norm to place the milk bottles at the front door, but rather to use the wooden gate marked "Tradesman's Entrance". Another prominently displayed mandate was "No hawkers and other lowly vendors allowed". It was very intriguing to my mind, finding an inpenetrable social barrier. What this intelligence conveyed to me was that I myself was meant by them to be confined to one strata of society, and whilst I would be tolerated to deliver their sustinence, my importance and value as a human being within the community would be severely restricted if I was to continue to regard myself as an equal member of their Society.

With the continuous back and fore 'twixt hoose and cairt, serving many different customers, it became apparent to me that there was a strong feeling of individualism and self importance demanding a high degree of attention to their all-imperative requirements. It was clear that Mr Peters had built up his business on the foonds of that old adage, "Impossibilities attended to immediately; miracles might take a little longer". I am afraid that the material or spiritual considerations for a minor cog in society such as myself were rather incidental. I quite believe that it was inconceivable for the wife of a man from the "professional classes" to take a mongrel dog in as a pet without being judged uncharitably by her peers, whilst exercising the animal, pedigree and the requirement to come from "good stock" being all-important.

Some households tried to vindicate their non-payment of bills. There was a strong undercurrent of money-meanness, but the further you penetrated the citadels of the West End this attitude differed a lot.

Mrs. D. McLaren.

16 Blenheim Place,
Aberdeen.

Some had a built-in barrier of isolation; they could have been living on the moon. Their intermediaries, often as not were "the skiffies", who mostly originated from the country, or had been especially trained for "service" by orphanages. As time passed by I heard many stories of how they suffered pure hell due to the treatment doled out to them by these so-called pillars of our city's "High Society". "Domestic Servant" may be an imposing title, but it seldom incurs tips. Christmas being for me "The Jackpot". That year (1930), I collected over £3·00 which meant that the festive season would be a merrier time for Dad and me. He could make good "clooty dumplings" and we both liked the long boxes of palm dates; none of this fare lasted long with us. Funds were further boosted by Harry Peters, the boss's son who would give me an extra shilling if I would stay after working hours and give the horses a currie comb and brush down at the mews behind No. 3 Osborne Place. Adam Strachan, my driver, who had at first appeared to be a sombre-minded man, turned out to be generous too and was good at slipping a tanner or two my way when times were tight.

Whilst my tips were left for me in an envelope marked "for the milkboy", it worried me what token of appreciation would be handed over to the servant quines; these orphaned lassies from the Poor Law Institutions. I shuddered to think what kind of Christmas they would have in the company of the religious bigots that were known to exist. What public good these so-called Christian people did was often-as-not overshadowed by a grave misuse of their responsibilities towards these unfortunates within the grey granite walls of their own stately homes. What does it profit such civic dignitaries and upholders of the established church if they "gain the whole world but lose their souls", never to learn from the "Man" who knew it all.

These people often did entertaining, and this meant extra work for these "skiffies" along with the usual household chores despite them rising before 5.30 a.m. to get the house spic and span ready for breakfast to be served on their master or mistress's table along with the preparation of a formal lunch. Along the line, some time, they were able to get some sort of a meal, but in many instances it was very plain and short in supply. Entertaining meant the thorough cleaning of the rooms; the setting out of tables and chairs; the cooking of special meals! For the welcoming and serving of guests, they had special dresses and starched accessories. It could be near midnight before these parties would finish, but it all had to be cleared up before they could drag their fatigued bodies up to their attic bedrooms which were usually small, and furnished in the Spartan style. The beds were either wooden-framed mangers or iron bedsteads; the steel straps bearing a flock mattress; probably one pillow, (feather) was supplied along with the bedsheets and a tawdry quilt. A skylight window relieved some of the gloom of this "poverty trap". I was often told that these household "captives" had less than I; they just couldn't afford to go anywhere. Many jobs were closed to women labour. The Victorian view that "a woman's place is in the home" made countless thousand bewail their lot in life. One house in particular, situated in The King's Gate District, had a reputation for greed and parsimony second to none. Every halfpenny was utilised with great caution, and it is my quiet contention that it was a fore-runner of the Concentration Camp System.

In direct contrast to this sheer hell, the bland replicas of its kidney, set amid manicured grounds of an awesome sameness about them, there was one gentleman's residence, who for every reason was a "Pillar" of the Toon; he bade at the end of Carlton Place, in the vicinity of Forest Avenue and Queen's Road Corners. I was impressed with the procedure that he requested I conformed to, namely that I was to make my way through an iron gate with no notice of any kind on it, up a gravel path to a flight of stone steps which I was to descend and gain access to the "below stairs" quarters of the house by means of a dark green door. There was a somewhat darkened hall inside where there was situated a long table with the empty bottles which I was to replenish. In his dealings with people from all walks of society, Mr Douglas was a Christian gentleman.

If the weather was bad, a few of the West End houses that I delivered to took you inside; into a warm kitchen where I was given a hot cup of cocoa accompanied by a bread and jam piece or a newly-baked scone spread with syrup. here cooks and servants could enjoy civilised employment. One such "Maister o' The Hoose" that I met was a well-known figure in the ship-building industry. He was a tall, thin, elderly man who was a bachelor. He had a good mind and used it especially where his staff were concerned. Another door that lit up in my world was at 16 Blenheim Place; a second floor flat where I delivered a pint of milk every day and eventually got to meet Mrs McLaren, a lady in every sense of the word; whose contact with and treatment of people confirmed to me what Jesus Christ had meant by exhorting his followers to give in full measure. The weather on the occasion of our first meeting had not been very good,

with alternating bouts of snow and rain, and the cold was intense. As she spoke to me, she took note that my clothing was less than desirable in order to keep me warm. She gave me mittens for my hands and asked about my home life, expressing genuine concern for my social welfare. Eventually she paid me a home visit and must have been appalled by the surroundings she found us in. She offered Dad help to put things a lot better, but knowing Dad, and his sense of independence, he refused this Christian help, but he did it in a mannerable, manly way, along with the utmost courtesy. Dad, as proud as he was, had a high-minded respect for her helping his son, which was offered as if it were the food and drink from "The Upper Room" itself. Mrs McLaren did not look on me as a prop by which means the divine order of things should be upheld. She didn't create communication barriers of a social, commercial, financial or political nature, and could equate with tragedies, privation, starvation and stark poverty. She had an inkling of the lifestyle of "the underlings"; the reason behind their flight to idleness, ignorance, a lack of ambition or a dullness of effort which they could only accept and regard as an "inheritance" from their forefathers. She regarded Privilege and Protocol as unimportant, even questioning why Wealth needed to be buttressed. She never allowed the "grand" spirit to adrenalise her way of thinking; maintaining that earthly-minded people were confused and guided by material values: Therein lay the seed of their sin. I mentally grasped then what Jesus meant by "the glory of the conquered" and "the spiritual victory over the world". Because Mrs McLaren could help me from "where she was at", Dad said that I could go to her house when I received a surprise invitation to visit her home for supper. Dad added "She seems to be a nice lady; nae mony o' them go aboot nowadays: If ye are tae ging, mind on to be clean and tidy. Be on your best behaviour and don't be gutsy. In this case, when ye go visiting there's nae need tae keep yer hat an' coat on; see fit I mean . . ."

Having gladly accepted her invitation to supper I rang their bell at the stated time of six o'clock. Presently Mr McLaren opened the door and invited me in. I was confronted by the grandeur of the entrance hall itself, that seemed to me the last word in luxury. The floor was covered with zig-zag lines in the floor surface which I learned later was "parquetry flooring". Two or three richly-patterned mats occupied the floor area. Not only was there a front door, but an inner door, with stained glass and etched panels of decoration in it. I was cordially escorted up two flights of carpeted stairs, whose treads were fixed in place by means of thick, shining brass rods, then on through the house door into a smaller hall which was fitted with lino and carpet. There was an umbrella stand and a row of wooden pegs for hats and coats to hang on. Mr McLaren then took me to meet his wife who was ready to receive me. The room was medium-sized, and to my young eyes appeared to be out of this world. I had never seen so many oil paintings and water colours, all encased in frames of ornate gold leaf, hanging in perfect unison from a wooden picture moulding by means of hook and chain. The square carpet was fixed to the floor with large brass carpet pins. The dining table, I noticed, was completely covered with a very nice spread; with plates and cutlery placed neatly for individual use. Around the table were six single chairs with back and seat upholstery; braided edges were craftsman-like, and brass antique nails were again in evidence. The sideboard looked over a hundred years old with opening doors at either side, and the central portion had four drawers with swan-neck drop handles. On the sideboard there was a big box holding cutlery for the table, and I noticed another container holding bottles of spirits. I found out that they called it a "tantalus"; what a lovely word it sounded to me. When I sat down to take my meal I could see that the rich velour curtains were lined with a self-coloured linen cloth; right round the top of the curtains was a deep pelmet, and hanging at each side of the window were ornate fancy tassels. I had always liked to look at the displays in the big furniture shops in Union Street such as J. & A. Ogilvie, Alexanders, Galloway & Sykes, and Roberts & Allan. My Uncle Rae was also an upholsterer with W. Brown & Sons of Union Street and The Hardgate. By speaking with Mrs McLaren the decision regarding my career was finally made.

The meal was tasty and went down well: a big plate of ham and eggs, butteries, bread, sandwiches, fancy biscuits and two cups of tea in the most delicate of china teacups. I was anxious that the handle would not disintegrate when I took a grip of it. The plates were exactly the same pattern.

Mr McLaren was a medium-sized elderly man with an engaging manner and enquiring mind. He asked me a lot of questions about myself and Dad. He hummed and heyed over some things to do with my answers, and I could tell that he had a "business" attitude; Mrs McLaren's eyes told me that I was alright. Mr McLaren had a military bearing and I found out that he had a close connection with The Boys' Brigade. Some time later I requested to use the W.C., (the word "bathroom" was never familiar to me). When I was shown in, everything in that room was in light green. I never had known such luxury existed. What entranced me was the press-down handle of the lavatory pot, the exquisite chromium hot and cold water taps, the delicate small plug of the wash hand basin. The bath itself was the most beautiful shaped thing that I had ever seen; the mirror was gilded, and there was a medicine cabinet. The small curtain swished on a metal track. There was a fixed metal tube for the heating and airing of all sorts of towels. There was a green sort of rubberised material on the floor but the pot and pedestals had carpets fitted around their bases.

Many boys like me brought up in the tenements didn't know about the existence of bathrooms within houses. Unlike the Arabs, we "Street Arabs" had no tents to fold and steal away to more fertile oases. It was refreshing to me however not to find on this occasion that slight intonation, which my hosts might have had towards my pals, seeping through. They didn't make me feel that they themselves were cast in a better mould; it was not the attention either that a pet dog might get. I was however fascinated by their psychology; did their ordered lives lack something; their roots embedded as they were in the sheer state of "having"; privilege that they may have acquired along with a richer background of material things, prudent thrift and educational superiority? I mulled over all these things; sad that I should at this tender age have such an old head on young shoulders, for I had come to question the needs of keeping their way of life for the successive generations. Although I admired the manner in which Mr and Mrs McLaren were able to give me an insight into their way of life I was on the lookout for flaws and imperfections that undermined the higher echelons of a society that had deprived my father of his war pension. I was thankful for the meal and the kindness shown to me, but I knew that the good Lord insisted that I couldn't dine at two tables.

Mrs McLaren however continued to be a welcome and staunch friend, encouraging me to better myself. I scoured the papers for alternative employment as a stepping stone to achieving my goal as an apprentice upholsterer, and I left Mr Peters to be a warehouse lad with Gordon & Graham, whisky & wine warehousemen and distillers in Market Street at somewhat short notice, I am afraid, for at interview they asked me if I could start immediately. Miss Euphemia Duncan and the foreman Hugh Webster issued me with a green apron; then I was handed a hard and soft brush, along with a tin of "Brasso" and soft cloth in order to give the firm's brass nameplates a high shine. I stuck in and polished them up so that they glinted and sparkled in the early morning sun. I had been aye vain enough to want to see my reflection gazing out at me as if it were encased in a sheet of gold. Up and down the length of Market Street I could hear the sound of continual jingling and the clashing of steel chain links, securely fixed on huge Clydesdale horses that plodded by; blurring images on the brass plate, like an early photographic image that I had noticed in the tramcar. The heavy iron shoes continued to make a tattoo of metallic noises on the greasy granite setts. The horses were urged to make the extra efforts for their masters; to pull in style and safety to ensure that their fellow steeds of burden could make it to the level of Union Street where the tracer horse was unyoked so that the same manoeuvres could be repeated nearly all day long. It was fascinating to hear the young drivers shouting encouragement whilst they were striving and heaving with exertion at some of the heavy loads behind them; made that much more difficult by the steep gradient of Market Street. I often noticed the pride and compassion with which these young drivers pulled the sweet sugar lumps from out of their pockets to give to their loyal charges; and the neighs of pleasure at their humble reward. This was an everyday scene that gave colour to a busy, thronging street. Presently, I was escorted downstairs to fill miniatures, gills and half bottles with whisky; I was also put on the screw tops; placing a plastic cup over the top of the bottle by means of compression in a rubber-encased vice. The final touch was a label and "wrap up". Other jobs included bottling port, sherry and claret, but the "big" job was to help Hughie make up the alcoholic density to the standard level required by the Government. At Christmas time, we worked an hour or two overtime, and I mind when we trooped upstairs from the workroom below, to where the general manager was standing at the front door. Mr Ballantyne was a rotund, middle-aged person with a bowler hat and regulation moustache; he oozed importance as he handed out packets of fags to the workers as they filed past him. When it came to my turn he remarked that I didn't smoke; and consequently his hand was withheld from me. It passed through my mind like a flash that "the labourer is worthy of his hire", and I hotly retorted that my Dad was a smoker. He gave me a sharp, hesitant glance, then as the winking of an eye, the cigarettes were in my hand. Fags at that time were eleven pennies for twenty. It was a false economy on his part, for I had unstintingly given his firm the use and value of my efforts. Must I be the loser?

On my errand duties around the immediate vicinity, I delivered whisky and wine to Flynn's Bar near the foot of Exchange Street. I often passed the Windsor Cafe, a rendezvous of doubtful characters; male and female, whose escapades were a continual source of trouble to the police and law-abiding citizens. My errands took me down to "The King's Highway", passing the empty, derelict remains of byegone tenements, where only the rats had domain. Friday was the day when The Green became alive with throngs of people edging their way through the cramped spaces that divided each stall selling their wares; especially eggs, butter and sowens as well as plentious supplies of country produce. Littlejohns, ships chandlers, had a shop here; further down near the Back Wynd Stairs, Adam the tea and coffee merchant had an emporium with an overhead sign, a giant-sized teapot.

The downstairs section of The New Market was wholly devoted to the selling of fish; all kinds of them, principally "the yellow haddie". Retracing my steps through the crowds in Hadden Street, I looked closely at the human parade and noticed a sameness of expression or direction in their faces and eyes. It became even more noticeable to me when I had to make a delivery of whisky and wine to "The Empire Bar" at the corner of Market Street and Guild Street. Large numbers of men were forming themselves into orderly queues that stretched down to Trinity Quay and were moving sure but slowly round the corner and up the steps of an official-looking building. It's lofty entrance seemed to devour them. As I drew nearer out of curiosity, I saw that they were filing into a long office where there was a continuous counter, and metal cages; inside which a white-collared worker was taking down notes. Once this process had been completed, the signing of official-looking papers took place, after which they were directed to wait on a long bench and were eventually summoned over to be handed money. This was my first experience of and contact with people of all sorts being paid dole money which would give them the meanest of excuses to survive in a midden of wartime, and even post wartime making. To me it was a tragic sight, these incorrigible crutches of human indignity; the spawning grounds and breeding processes of all as yet uncommitted forms of crime. So this was the metronome that balanced and separated the lifestyles of certain human beings.

To my untried mind this image created a mental and moral horror. Who was Anti-Christ amid God's world that continually could legislate millions of God's people into dire straits of poverty; deciding how little money these unfortunate families could perhaps exist on in Aberdeen and throughout the nation? I also saw, (with hindsight), that these men carried cards and were franked with a Government stamp which kept them in insurance benefit. It was a common sight to see a lot of men, who had probably been standing in their queues of iniquity for a long time to show their franked cards to one another; even joking about it, but there was a flat, graceless ring to their repartees. The .frayed clothing, the patched shoes or boots didn't escape my notice. The silent ones were having a thoughtful puff of a Woodbine cigarette which they never finished; snibbing it, then putting the "tabbie" in a little tobacco tin to provide a smoke later in the day.

Retracing my steps past the impassive facade of The New Market, I passed under the archway at the top of Market Street in order to have a keek into the window of Burton, "The Fifty Shilling Tailors"; their suits were made of "Botany" wool. (I knew how they were, as I had bought my first suit there at one of their sales, for thirty five shillings; it lasted me on and off for over ten years).

When Mrs McLaren paid me a surprise visit to find out how my search for alternative employment was progressing, I wasn't sure as I answered the door how Dad would react to the presence of a woman in the house; especially a woman wearing a fur coat, for since Mum and Grandma Duncan had died he only permitted his nieces over the threshold. My friend was well groomed, her grey hair simply but elegantly cut, and deep in her eyes I noticed a zest for living. As I could not keep her standing there, I let her in, and she stepped forward effortlessly in her sensible shoes. Dad hadn't heard us, for he was sitting in his shirtsleeves deep in concentration with a George Gissing novel. His back was to us; the horizontal splats of the country-made kitchen chair forming a flag-like pattern with his galasses and the ticking pattern expanse of his collarless shirt. The curtains, were as a rule, almost drawn. This gave the house an atmosphere of continuous twilight. Dad held the book close up to his face, for his eyesight had been seriously impaired when he was serving his country in France at the Battle of Cambrai. Even yet, his eyes were continually red-rimmed due to the after-effects of mustard gas intake. He also seemed to be continually under fire night and day from a wracking cough due to his lungs, throat and vocal chords likewise being corroded by the mustard gas. (The Medical Commission), a year after the event examined him again and lightly passed off his maladies as a form of bronchitis and thereby terminated his war pension. This high-handed decision had further rankled his hot-quick temper and stubborn streak. The shrapnel splinters were still present, embedded in the side of his skull. Consequently he found himself in the battlefront of marital relationships. The death of his brother David, a regular soldier serving in The Gordon Highlanders at the Battle of Mons left his mother alone and handicapped. He retreated from Mum and us to carry out his filial duty. He saw to it that the strength of mental power that he thereby attained was passed on to me as soon as I was impressionable; this was the bond between us: the ability to plead our cause with fellow human beings, irrespective of clan or creed. Before that moment of encounter, I understood the look of apprehension and mingled compassion on Mrs McLaren's normally placid face.

Mrs McLaren promptly explained her presence of course as he swung round, and I was relieved that she could draw him out of himself and have eye contact communication with him. Dad was hesitant in his conversation at first; he suddenly appeared to be self-conscious of his powerful hands that had been so accustomed to the rigours of the welding trade, and now were stilled; no longer to be skilfully used due to his injuries. He continued to insolently pick at his hoary finger nails which required clipping, for he had discarded the novel; however, his studied politeness and formality which he carried almost to the point of open wariness of our West End visitor melted when he had finally gauged how perceptive and genuine she was in the way she mouthed the inner feelings of her heart and mind when I was the subject of discussion.

She was the harbinger of good news, and had been able to arrange an interview for me as a prospective apprentice upholsterer with the bosses of J. & A. Ogilvie, the top furniture shop in Union Street. I was to report to the bosses, Mr Skea and Mr Forbes.

Next day I requested leave to attend for an interview with J. & A. Ogilvie and explained my plans for an apprenticeship to Hughie Webster, who turned out to be a good friend and helper. In fact he gave me permission to go without loss of pay. When the time came, I was spick and span, guaranteed to pass muster by any sergeant-major, on any parade ground. The interview itself was very thorough too, but the kind offices of Mrs McLaren had tilted it to my advantage. I was told that I should start on the Monday morning following, at 8 a.m., and report to their Mr Grainger. To start with, I would have to do a stint on the work lift; keep it in working order and book in all goods on arrival at the loading bay. My remuneration was nine shillings and sixpence a week. It was considered to be a good wage for a young working man in 1931, and I was walking on air; full of excitement, wondering at my good luck.

As I returned to hand in my notice at Market Street, I took the Windmill Brae route, over the railway brig to The Green, and I began to see my surroundings in a different dimension. Although this particular district had been besmirched by the reputation of "the blue ointment" and "the condom", the city did after all grow up on the wattle, splintered wood and refuse of other generations; and although the original dwellers of the inner city tenements were in large numbers being thrust to the outskirts, where new council estates were arising on virgin farmland, the lives and customs of our immediate forefathers would in some measure survive the inroads of the archaeologically destructive pile-driver. I wondered then, as I indeed do now, whether we will gain greater sense to sink some money, however paltry the sum, in order to safeguard our oral history and traditions. Time alone is the decider, and the judge.

ORIGIN OF THE ABERDEEN DIALECT

The Aberdeen doric, if you can call it that, is not something belonging to Aberdeen as a single entity; it has never been a preserve of its people.

It could be likened to a quilt patchwork form of speech, incorporating the fisher folk, the farm worker, the "gang aboot bodies" and the heritage of gone-by immigrants of Nordic or Flemish extraction. They little knew that this volcanic potency of words would have such far-reaching effects in formal literature and daily expression, thereby allowing the vocabulary of the ethnic Aberdonian to increase

its kinetic qualities and dual meaning. Frontiers were pushed forward by the Gaelic influences, and assimilation of elements of their language and philosophies eased the growing pains of this city. Thus a sound in common was consolidated, so that they could converse with and understand one another as fellow citizens. What makes the Aberdeen mode, (characteristic way of speaking), so superlative, is that the intonation can be changed from the slow, cautious, penetrating way of asking something and confirming it at the same time. This is an established habit, ingrained as bone marrow itself; keen with of those whose strength of mind wrested a living from the soil. Words of wisdom like a flash of inspiration from Mother Nature herself; employing short, sharp syllabic bursts — a psychological hurling of javelins at each other.

This was a way of life that exposed the sharp wit and intellect of the trader, keeping him in fighting form, as if he was continually selling his wares on the market place. This modus operandi was animated with the vulgar, earthy patter of people battling to withstand or overcome the primitive and impoverished way of the hovel and the filth of "The Vennel".

The dialect of the Aberdonian may have changed as the way of life developed in the differing climate of industry or commerce; but the basic roots of speech remained, displaying the solid qualities of its native granite.

The vandals, who have in large diluted this unique form of conversation, were the creators of the new housing estates, tearing up the roots as well as the habitat of generations. In this sense the price paid for the improvements to our general standard of living was an inordinately high one.

Moreover, the real criminals of our birthright were comedians and other preditors, who even yet demean and poke fun at the lifestyle and diction of East End citizens. The Aberdonian with his accent will survive all their paradies and would-be-betrayals. However folk prefer the simple gesture of quietly opening their homes and hearts to the many strangers who knock at their door, and take pride in subsequently making them their children. The rare virtue of such Aberdonians is the ability to assimilate the changing scene; to use it for survival in one sense, and gaining in another way the means of crossing cosmopolitan frontiers without having recourse to "special privilege"; taking a pride in being "educationally and socially acceptable".

ABERDEEN MY CITY

Aiberdeen, grey granite toun:
mica like uncut diamonds; untelt siller aroun'.
Sullen herbour waters scourin' the muckle steens,
an' win' caul-snell gnawin' at the marrow o' oor beens.

Aiberdeen, grey granite toun:
loo'ed by quine an' orra loun;
peerin' doon at but an' ben
in a wye the Varsity professors 'll never ken.

Aiberdeen, grey granite toun:
that claimed the first photie o' the moon.
Her wark force fechtin' the ootside warld as a hale;
yestreen the prood iron prow, the clippers' sail.

Aiberdeen, grey granite toun:
aye enduring, faimily an' foon';
aul' freens through the thranging years
"Granite City" o' couthy peers.

Aiberdeen, grey granite toun:
wing span o' tenements awa owre soon.
Mosses and lichens on granite seldom grow,
wi' my clicketty clackitty gird, doon Memory Lane
    I will go.

Aiberdeen, grey granite toun:
whaur Childhood's chairies were once a boon:
in adult life the landmarks they have become,
be it "The Spiralled City", or a brookit lum.

Aiberdeen, grey granite toun:
whaur the leerie o' Local History treads saftly, wi'oot
    a soun';
Lichtin' his Lampie o' Learnin' nae oor sicht tae impair—
in a' the guid places, whaur we can be nae mair.

Forestairs at The Hardweird.

OOR FOWK; THEIR FOWK; ONY FOWK

Here's tae a' yer fowk
An' oor fowk an' a' the fowk
That likes oor fowk an' yer fowk;
I wunner what ails fowk at fowk
That fowk winna lat fowk like fowk?
If fowk wad lat fowk like fowk,
Fowk wud like fowk as weel
As fowk ever did like fowk.

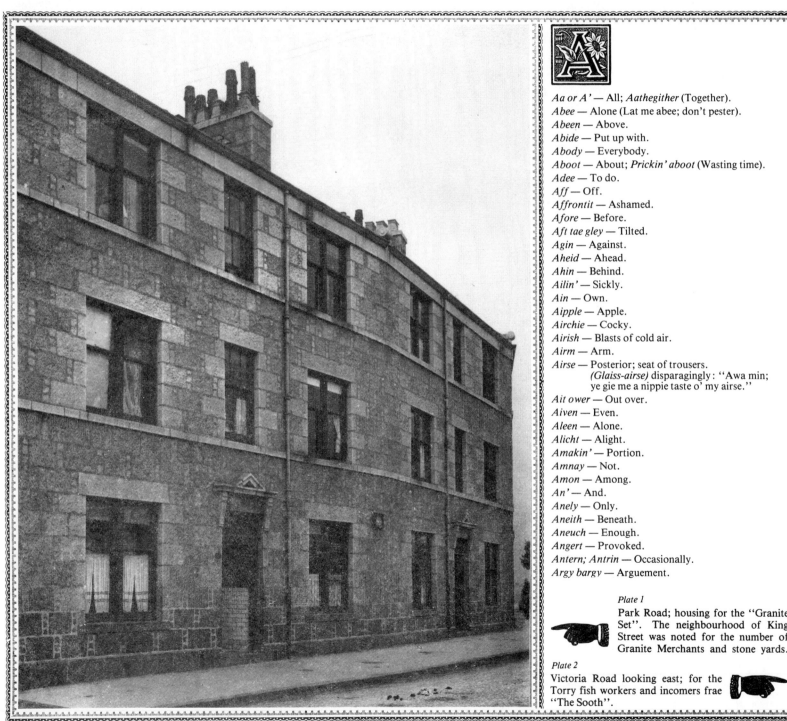

Aa or A' — All; *Aathegither* (Together).

Abee — Alone (Lat me abee; don't pester).

Abeen — Above.

Abide — Put up with.

Abody — Everybody.

Aboot — About; *Prickin' aboot* (Wasting time).

Adee — To do.

Aff — Off.

Affrontit — Ashamed.

Afore — Before.

Aft tae gley — Tilted.

Agin — Against.

Aheid — Ahead.

Ahin — Behind.

Ailin' — Sickly.

Ain — Own.

Aipple — Apple.

Airchie — Cocky.

Airish — Blasts of cold air.

Airm — Arm.

Airse — Posterior; seat of trousers.
(Glaiss-airse) disparagingly: "Awa min; ye gie me a nippie taste o' my airse."

Ait ower — Out over.

Aiven — Even.

Aleen — Alone.

Alicht — Alight.

Amakin' — Portion.

Amnay — Not.

Amon — Among.

An' — And.

Anely — Only.

Aneith — Beneath.

Aneuch — Enough.

Angert — Provoked.

Antern; Antrin — Occasionally.

Argy bargy — Arguement.

Plate 1

Park Road; housing for the "Granite Set". The neighbourhood of King Street was noted for the number of Granite Merchants and stone yards.

Plate 2

Victoria Road looking east; for the Torry fish workers and incomers frae "The Sooth".

42

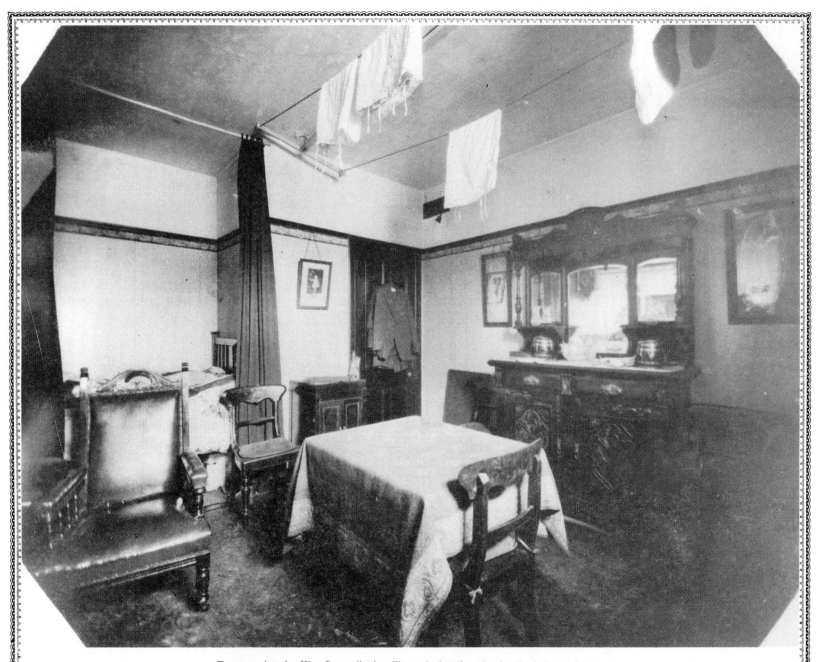

Plate 3   Tenement interior King Street district: Fitewashed reefs, ochred wa's (ha' wye doon), varnished wa'paper the rest a'roun'; lino on the fleer, "bitties o' sticks tae furnish a room. (N.B. bed recess; there were no bathrooms, even in the more middle-class apartments).

Plate 4   Tenement interior Rosemount district: Pulley an' picturies fixed tae the wa'; a gas licht by which tae see it a': Chairies drawn up tae the glimmerin' fire, bilin' kettlie an' a fender bra'. I min' us a' gaitherin' aroun' the fireside at nicht; the gas jets turned doon low, telling ghaist stories. It was a Friday nicht jobbie tae scrub the steel fender wi' carbolic soap, then polish it until it shone in a dull kind o' wye.

Plate 5
Backie in the Rosemount district: Lavie on the stairs an' lang windae on the landin'; baith, a tenant's
dream. Cellars an' palings trim; an' yer week's washin' hingin' clean.

Plate 7
Tenement hoosies, mickle an' muckle: Leadside Road looking towards "The Tower", a baronial pile for artizans on the corner of Short Loanings.

A'richt — Alright.
Aroon — Around.
Arrant — Complete.
Atween — Between.
Aucht nor oucht — Nothing at all; (neither one thing or the other).
Aul — Old; *Aul'eens* (Anything old).
Aul farrant — Nosey.
Ava — At all.
Awa — Gone.
A weers o' — On point of.
Awfu' — Awful.
Aye — Always.
Ayint — Beyond; Past.

Plate 6
Rosemount Place: "The flooer amang them a'; wi' The Co-opie Shops, Murdoch's rolls, an' fruiterers' shoppies een or twa.

Bauchles — Old shoes.
Back birn — A load carried on the shoulders.
Backies — Drying greens.
Backit — Refuse bin.
Bade — Stayed.
Baffies — Carpet slippers.
Bairn — Child; *Bairny* (Adult childish in a certain way).
Baith — Both.
Bakeit — Baked.
Bamstick — Useless person.
Bandy — Young fish.
Beens — Bones.
Bannock — Oatmeal pancakes cooked on a gridle.

Bap — Scone made with butter.
Barfit — Barefoot.
Barkit — Skinned.
Baskettie — A wee basket.
Bawbee — Halfpenny.
Beddit — Bedded down.
Beerit — Buried.
Beets — Boots.
Behouchie — Behind.
Beiling — Blister, Whitlow.
Belang — Belong.
Bellas — Bellows.
Bender — Drinking spree.
Ben the hoose — Inner part of the house.
Beock — Vomit.
Besom — Broom made of heather.
Beuk — Book.
Bigsie — Conceited.
Bikky — Bitch.

Plate 8
Filly and colt; townhorses stabled and trained in Short Loanings by Mr Courage.

The Hardweird looking towards Jack's Brae: Forestairs, fish hakes an' fun an' games.

Plate 10

Biler — Boiler; wash-house or street tar boiler; inferring old-fashioned ways.
Billy — Fellow; Companion, i.e. "Bothy Billy".
Birkie — Lively fellow.
Birled — Rotating at a pace.
Birr — Vigour.
Birse — Bristle.
Birse Cup — Cup of tea laced with whisky — a beverage named after the Feuchside Parish of that name.

Plate 9

Below: Mr England's Coalstore in Short Loanings. He wis the sweepie an' the coalmannie.

Birstlin' — Roasting.
Blaa-oot — A big row.
Black-affrontit — Shamed to death.
Blad — Soiled.
Blake — Grimey person.
Blate — Bleat; Shy.
Bleed-jeelin' — Blood coagulating.
Bleeze — Blaze; *Bleezin'* (Drunk).
Blether — Chatter.
Blicht — Blight.
Blicker — Tarnished, even scittery matter.
Blin' — Blind.
Blue keek — Black eye.
Bocht — Purchased.
Bogie — Small trailer; Carriage.
Bookies' runner — Street corner operator.
Boo' it — Bowed.
Bools — Game of glass or clay marbles.
Boord — Board.
Bosie — Bosom hug; *Bosie doon* (Go to sleep).
Boorachie — Heap; Knot of people.
Bowster — Bolster.
Boxie — Small box, "A nackie wee box".
Brae — Road with a steep gradient; Hillside.
Braid — Broad.

Braig — Brag.
Braith — Breath.
Brak — Break.
Brat — Worker's coarse-spun apron.
Bree — Juice.
Breem — Broom.
Breenge — Jump forward.
Breid — Bread.
Breist — Breast.
Bricht — Bright.
Britchen — Breeching (Harness on a breech of horses).
Brither — Brother.
Broch — Fraserburgh.
Brookit — Covered with soot.
Broon — Brown.
Brose — Oatmeal or peasmeal, mixed with either of the following: Hot milk, butter, salt, brosy, stout.
Brunt — Burned.
Bubblyjock — Turkey cock.
Buckie — Welk.
Buff — Idle talk.
Buroo — Bureau; Unemployment Exchange.
Buttery — High fat roll.

Plate 11
Jack's Brae an' the bedding factory lookin' north: Reteasin' horsehair, teezin' flechs that teased the people.

Plate 13
Right: Jack's Brae and March Lane looking towards Skene Street School: Snuffy noses, six a bed, big nail tae hing claes ahin' the door.

Plate 12
Below: Hipped reef, hurley, an' The Huntly Street Co-opie.

Leerie's extension ladders.

Plate 15

Left: Skene Street looking east from Chapel Street, (northern end now truncated). Peat-smoke, pends an' chocolate fondant pipes. I wis born at 113 Skene Street. Fae Skene Street tae Minister Lane wis only a flight o' stane steppies awa'.

Plate 14

Below: Bookie's runner, beer money an' wife batterin'. The Denburn lookin' towards South Mount Street and the "hammer blocked", coursed and ashlar facades 1887-1900 (Aberdeen Extension & Improvement Act (1883), the new entry to the city from Rosemount).

Plate 17

Right: Denburn looking towards Stevenson Street in 1930; there were 447 insanitary dwellings in this district. Overcrowding, cock lafts an' Skene Street School. This aul' hoose hiz seen mair than "The Swine's Closie". She kent the sicht o' Jimmy The Scaffie an' Ivan The Russian, (but he never said muckle).

Plate 16

Below: Richmond Street looking south: cold, hard and treeless, canned herring for the army; cassies an' corner shoppies. The Back-to-back tenements date from c.1875. The factory later became H. W. Hunter's furniture stores but was burnt out in 1937; "Rosemount Square" occupies the site.

Caal — Cold.
Ca away — Carry on by all means.
Ca through — Pull through.
Cack — Excrete;
    Cack up — (Urge on).
Cairds — Playing cards.
Cairtie — 4 Wheeled children's cart.
Caker — Easy job.
Caller — Cool; fresh.

Cankert — Ill-natured.
Canle — Candle.
Cannylike — Gently; careful.
Cantrip — Joke.
Cappie — Ice cream cone.
Carcage — Carcass.
Carle — Churl; *Carline* (Rough
    vociferous wifie).
Cassen oot — Cast out.
Cassies — Setts; granite street blocks.
Caul' — Cold.
Caup — Wooden "brose bowl"
    generally on sale at "The
    Timmer Market".

Plate 19

Plate 18
("Low") Skene Street an' Black's Buildings : Black by name; bruickit by nature.

Plate 19

Black smoke fae the trains sooted Blackfriars Street. On the right is the "Art Gallery and Industrial Museum". Cowdray Hall now has replaced the tenements with loftier sentiments: (The War Memorial).

Plate 20

Craigie Street Backies : Peeling hoardings, peeling paint an' peelie-wallies; (even with the use of 'Abdine' powders, as advertised).

My home in St. Andrew Street, and the corner o' Crooked Lane: Bedridden, bed bugs an' bad dreams. Pupils who attended The Demonstration School here were kent as "The Demi Duds". I learnt too soon that "The Warld is a toon wi' mony crookit wyes; an' Death is a mercat place whaur a' fowk gaither. If Life wis a' fancy gear that fowk aye hanker aifter; the man wi' the siller wid be able tae bide; noo his peer brither is jist wearin' awa".

Plate 21

Chack — Chalk; blue and white chequered linen or calico cloth.

Chaffs — Jaws.

Chanter — Practise chanter (bagpipes).

Chape — Cheap.

Chappit — Chopped up potato or turnip; lips so affected by hard frost.

Checker — Cinema attendant.

Cheep — Whisper.

Cheerie — Chair.

Chiel — Hardy man.

Chippit — Squashed, or bruised.

Chock — Choke.

Chore — Act of thieving.

Chraichly host — Bad cough.

Chuckies — Small granite pebbles.

Chunty — Chamber pot.

Cickie — Cack; excrete.

Claer — Correct; distinct.

Claes — Clothes.

Claik — Gossip; *Claikit* (Idly tattled).

Clapdarnack — Dried excrement.

Clapper — Wooden rattle.

Clarty — Dirty.

Clatter — Noise.

Clench — Limp.

Click — Find a sweetheart.

Clockie — Gill of whisky in a round bottle.

Clockin' — Brooding.

Cloggies — Sawn-off firewood.

Plate 22

Harriet Street Backies: "Brockeners", brokers, an' "The Harriet Street Bar". (Wordie's Stables occupied the backland on the eastern side of the street, with access from Ross' Court Schoolhill and "Little" Loch Street. Mutter & Howie also had extensive stables in Charlotte Street, and these were approached by means of a ramp).

Plate 23

Robertson's "Queen's Corner Shop", (later Reith Bros. an' noo Marks & Spencer): St. Nicholas Street, looking north; the view is noo obscured by "The St. Nicholas Centre". Dad told me that a relation from The Royal Burgh o' Inverurie, a mason by the name of George Duncan, had sculpted the plinth for the bronze effigy of old Queen Victoria, remarking somewhat coldly that she "wis jist anither customer". Famous emporiums he approved of were Robertson's the Clothiers, an' Raggie Morrison's in the Netherkirkgate nearby; an' a dash o' "The Lemon Tree Bar", opposite.

58

Clook — Claw.

Clorach — Untidy.

Clort — Ill-dressed woman.

Closie — Common stair access to
      tenements.

Clootie — Cloth; rag (put around a
      fruit dumpling).

Clour — Strike; dent.
      Clooert (Battered).

Clype — Tell-tale; ("Clypie-clashy pan").

Cock-Fillet — Slating technique,
      i.e. "Cock lafts".

Cockle-eyed — Twisted eyes; squint.

Combees — Combinations.

Con feerin' — Consonant to.

Confuffled — Confused.

Connached — Muck-up.

Conter'd — Contradicted.

Contermashious — Contrary.

Coorse — Coarse; wicked.

Corbie — Crow.

Coup — Upset or overturn.

Couthy — Homely.

Crabbit — Ill-tempered; greetin'-faced.

Crack — Talk.

Cracket — Cracked.

Craft — Croft.

Craichly — Catarrhal.

Crannie — Little finger.

Crappie — Stomach.

Cratur — Creature or person down
      on his luck; (deserving of pity).

Crood — Crowd.

Crookit — Bent.

Croon — Crown.

Crop — Haircut.

Cuddie — Donkey.

Cuppie — Cup.

Curn — Small amount; (Curnies).

Cyaird — Brawling, swearing
      woman. *Plate 24*

Upperkirkgate lookin' east: Grant's Court, ghaists, a' ging their gate. The physic, Rachel Joss (née Johnston) lived in rooms over A. B. Hutcheson's baker shop; she had no need to open doors as poltergeists were constantly in attendance. She hoped that nobody else would have to bide there after her, and that the place would be pulled down. Nobody did; and it was accordingly eradicated. The street-line has been taken back, and "St. Nicholas Centre" has replaced the open space which was left behind.

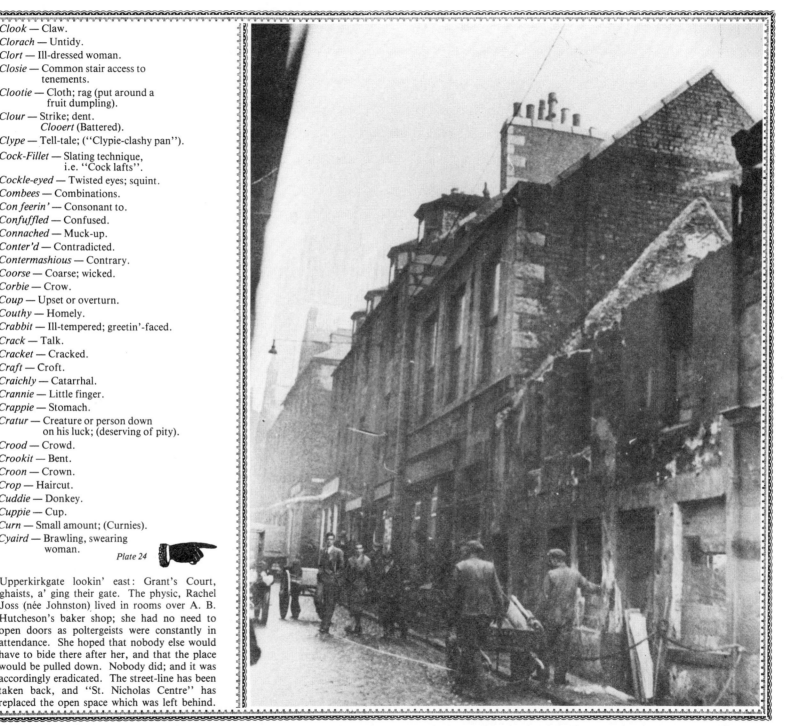

Dadd — Strike.

Dae — Do.

Daith — Death.

Dander — Saunter.

Deem — Dame; (She's a big deem).

Deid — Dead.

Deil — Devil.

Delse — Seaweed delicacy.

Dementit — Mad; unreasonable.

Denner — Dinner.

Dickie — Starch collar and shirt front.

Dicted — Wiped up.

Didnae — Didn't?

Ding — Ring true. (Ding-on — To
rain or snow).

Dinna — Do not.

Dird — Drive (or cast violently).

Dirk — Dagger.

Dirler — Chamber pot. (Dirling —
Stinging; rotating).

Dish cloot — Dish cloth.

Div — Do.

Divot — Flat turf.

Dochter — Daughter.

Docken — Leaf with healing
properties especially for blisters.

Dook — Bathe.

Doitit — Stupid.

Dollop — Dubbie.

Doon — Down.

Doot — Doubt.

Dottl't — Confused.

Dour — Silent; (As dour as the devil
and as blithe as a bride).

Dowp — Bottom.

Dram — Glass of whisky.

Drap — Drop; (Ye've drappit yer
false teeth intae the nicht utensil).

Drate — Excrete.

 Plate 25

Barnett's Close looking towards Guestrow from
Flourmill Lane: Dispensary, drugs and adrenalin.
The Dispensary occupied premises here, (left),
1871-1900, moving to 25 Castle Street thereafter.
It was said that the removal of The Dispensary
would be little short of disaster to Aberdeen.

Plate 26   Thornton Place (No. 29); Thornton Court (No. 37). Baith cheek by jowl in "The Gush". (Demolished circa 1932).   Plate 27

Guestrow lookin' north: The Gush an' its gentlemen, gone with the echo o' the clickitty clackitty girds.

Plate 28

Dreich — Damp; misty cold.

Droon — Drown.

Drooth — Heavy drinker; thirst.

Droukit — Soaked.

Dubs — Mud.

Duddies — Rags; rough kind of clothes.

Dudgicks — Sunday best suit (Braws).

Dulse — Heated seaweed, (delicacy).

Dumb-foonert — Amazed at some- one's patter.

Dunt — Blow or knock; (*Pay on the dunt;* otherwise promptly).

Dwam — Dream.

Dyker — Builder of rough stone hedges.

Dyste — Stamp or thump.

Eck — Contraction for Christian name Alexander.

Edick — Edict.

Ee — Eye; wall-eyed (starey eyed).

Eident — Busy.

Eik — Make an addition.

Ense — Otherwise.

Errans — Errands.

Evnoo — Just now.

Hand Cairt.

Plate 29

Plate 30

Charles Court, 44 Upperkirkgate; Milner's Court, 25 Guestrow (demolished c.1932). (Twa courts tae dee wi' ''The Stewart Laddie'', (Charles II), an' ''The Butcher'', The Duke o' Cumberland, who stabled his horses here, from September 1745 to April 1746). ''Cumberland Hoose'', (now Provost Skene's Mansion), wis itself scheduled for destruction in 1934.

64

Plate 32
Shiprow Reefs lookin' towards the Fish Mercat an' The Herbour : Chimney pots, pantiles, and chunty pots.
Owners of battered ''moleskins'' considered bleachgreens to be a luxury in this neighbourhood.

Plate 33

"The Damp Closie"; aul' claes hingin' on lang poles; the peat sheddies are doon noo, (the site of ABC Cinema car park). The fit o' St. Katherine Hill wis weel kent as "The Whore's Dyke" district o' Aiberdeen.

Plate 34

Commerce Street, (southern end); "The smallest hoose in Aiberdeen"; even so, it was occupied by two families; (the inside staircase was on the sharpside). The smallest shop in the city still survives in Millburn Street; it was originally a bagpipe dealer's premises. Another "Hole in the wa'" is "Aladdin's Cave", an antique shop at 37½ Skene Square.

Fa — Who.

Fa' — Fall.

Fae — From.

Faggot — Unruly woman.

Fairfochen — Thirsty; dry.

Fankle — Muddle; snarl.

Farin' — Getting on.

Fash — Worry; vex; bother unduly.

Fashious — Peevish.

Faurer — Farther.

Feart — Afraid.

Fechts — Arguments.

Feckless — Weak.

Fee — Period of agricultural employment (Feein' Market in Aberdeen).

Feel — Daft.

Feuch — Whiff.

Fibber — Teller of lies.

Fleck — Flea.

Flee the doo — Up and away; take to your heels.

Flisty — Moment.

Flit — Move.

Floo'r — Flower.

Flycup — Cup o' tea accompanied by "a piece", biscuit etc.

Flytie — Changeable.

Foo — *How much.*

Foolmach — Scarlet (or dirty woman).

Foostie — Stale.

Footrick — Awkward person.

Forbye — By the way.

Forrit — Forward.

Founert — Exhausted.

Founs — Foundations.

Fowk — People.

Froon — Frown.

Frostit — Frosted.

Fu' — Full.

Fule — Fool.

Fusionless Footer — Person with no strength.

Fut — What.

Fylie — Little while.

 Plate 35

Long Acre looking westwards towards Marischal College: Bedclothes dryin', slum street dyin'; little girl sighin'.

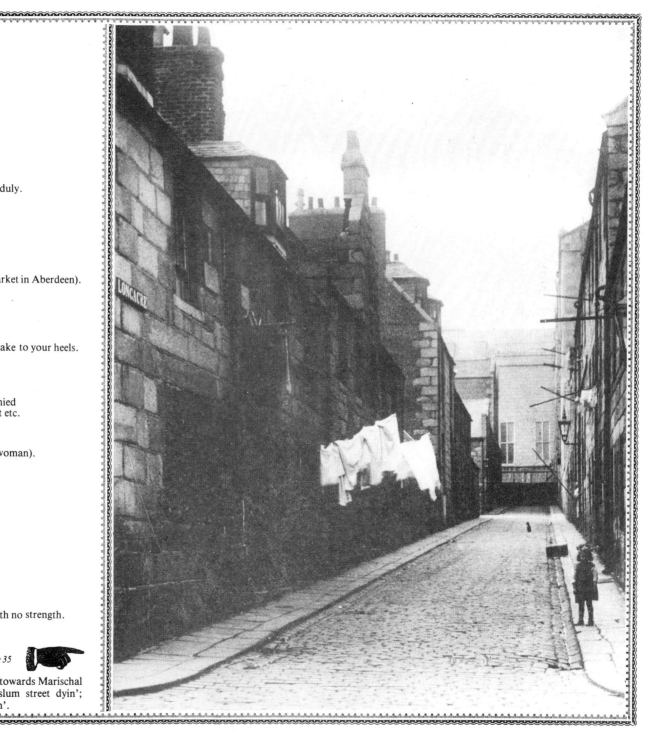

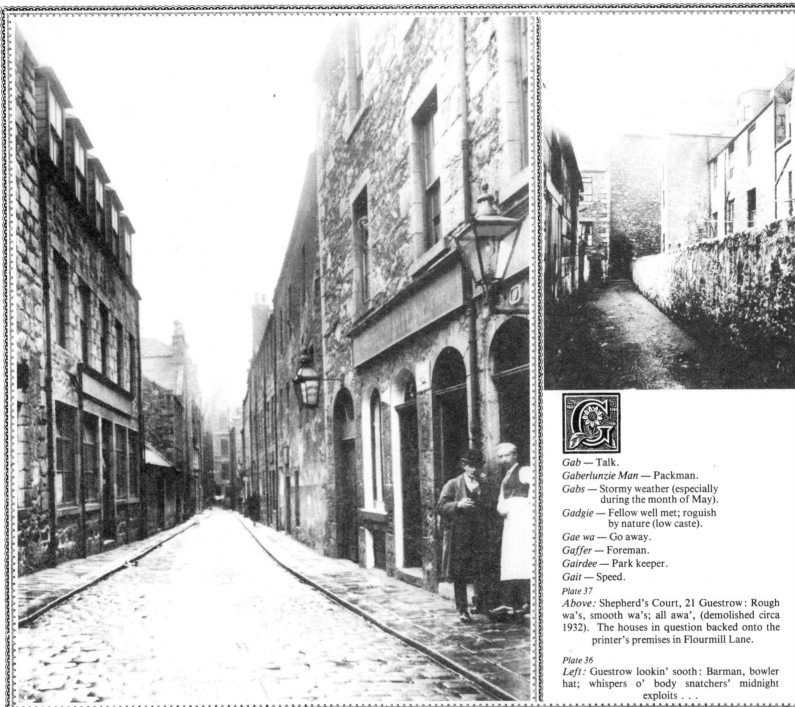

Gab — Talk.

Gaberlunzie Man — Packman.

Gabs — Stormy weather (especially during the month of May).

Gadgie — Fellow well met; roguish by nature (low caste).

Gae wa — Go away.

Gaffer — Foreman.

Gairdee — Park keeper.

Gait — Speed.

Plate 37

Above: Shepherd's Court, 21 Guestrow: Rough wa's, smooth wa's; all awa', (demolished circa 1932). The houses in question backed onto the printer's premises in Flourmill Lane.

Plate 36

Left: Guestrow lookin' sooth: Barman, bowler hat; whispers o' body snatchers' midnight exploits . . .

Shuttle Lane from Shuttle Court: Poachers, tattie pickers, an' poltergeists. Cottages here had nae grun' at the back, an' were aye bein' closed by "the Sanitary Department Mannie". One particular attic room had hardly been condemned, when heavy footsteps were heard in the room below, that couldn't be explained awa'; even the fleerboards creaked wi' an unkent wecht. [The manifestations ceased as abruptly as they had started on January 20th, 1933. The Society for Psychic Research had sometimes been in attendance until 4 a.m. investigating].

Plate 38

Gallasses — Braces.

Gallivantin - Jaunt.

Gammy — Injured.

Gang — Go.

Gangrel — Man of the road.

Ganzie — Roll-knecked jersey worn by fisher folk.

Gapit — Gaped.

Gar — Compel; cause.

Garn — Work.

Garret — Top room ; attic.

Gart — Made.

Gast — Sudden fright.

Gaun'-aboot Bodie — Tramp; pikie; person at a loose end.

Gawket — Awkward.

Gazunder — Chamber pot.

Gean Tree — Wild cherry.

Gear — Property.

Geets — Brat of a child; infant.

Gey Hard Ca'd — Hardworked.

Gey Ticht — Greedy.

Gie Billie — High spirited man.

Gie keek — Good look; sex appeal inferred.

Gie mochie — Dim; misty.

Gie smert — Clever.

Gilpin — Simple person.

Gin — If.

Ging — To go.

Gipe — Idiot.

Gas Service truck.

Gird — Barrel hoop.
Girdle — Iron plate for baking.
Girn — Complaining and whining.
Girse — *Grass.*
Glaiket — Stupid.
Gless — Glass.
Glim — Small light.
Gloamin' — Twilight.
Glye-eyed — Squint eye.
Gomeril — Fool.
Goon — Gown.
Gowk — Fool; *Gowkit* (Foolish).
Grafting — Working hard.
Grass Hopper — Peeping Tom.
Greetin' — Crying; *Grat* (Wept).
Grippie — Mean.
Grist — Corn.
Growthe — Weeds.
Grun' — Ground.

Haar — Cold mist.
Habber — Stammer.
Hach — Clear the throat.
Hack — Notch; *Hacks* (Cuts sustained to hands by frost): *(Hackit han's).* (Disparagingly referring to a prostitute).
Haddicks — Haddock; (Haddies).
Hae — Have.
Haggert — Cut ragged.
Haik — Gossiping female.
Hairst — Harvest.
Haive — Throw.
Haiver — Talk foolishly.

 Plate 39

Blairton Lane and Cheynes (Broad Street to Guestrow) . . . now a "clean sweep". If ye had jist left school an' there wis nae jobbie tae ging til ye went to "The Buroo School" in Broad Street so that yer Da wid get the allowance o' twa shillings. A customer at a grocer's shoppie in "The Gush", asked for his "twa sheaves o' loaf" to be cut langwyes alang the loaf for tippence.

Hake — Triangular wooden frame with hooks for the purpose of drying fish.
Halesome — Healthy.
Halla — Hollow.
Hallirackit — Hoydenish.
Hameower — Homely.
Han' fu' — Handful.
Hanless — Useless.
Haps — Covers; *Hapit* (Covered).
Harns — Brains.
Hash — Hurried; (Rough work).
Haud — Hold.
Hauf — Half.
Havering — Undecided; blethering rubbish.
Havers — Nonsense.
Headdie — Headmaster.
Heedin' — Paying attention to.
Heest — Hasten.
Heicht — Hight.
Heid — Head; (Baheid: Round ball filled with air). (Beastie heid: Lice).
Heistin' — Hoisting.
Hemmer — Hammer.
Herm — Harm.
Hert — Heart.
Hertnin' — Encouragement.
Het — Hot.
Hey min — Hello.
Hick — High temper.
Hicht — Height; (Jimpin' his ain hicht).
Hine awa — A long way away. (Awa hinie).
Hing — Hang: Jist hingin' thegither. (Hing in till ye hing oot).
Hinmist — Last.
Hinnae — Have not.
Hinner — Hinder.
Hippens — Old cloots cut up and used as nappies.

Shoe Lane looking westwards towards Greyfriars Kirk, and eastwards to West North Street and Chronicle Lane. The hoosies on the northern side of Shoe Lane, (later St. K's Club), were jist pairt o' this "doon at heel" neebourhood . . .

Plate 40a

Plate 40b

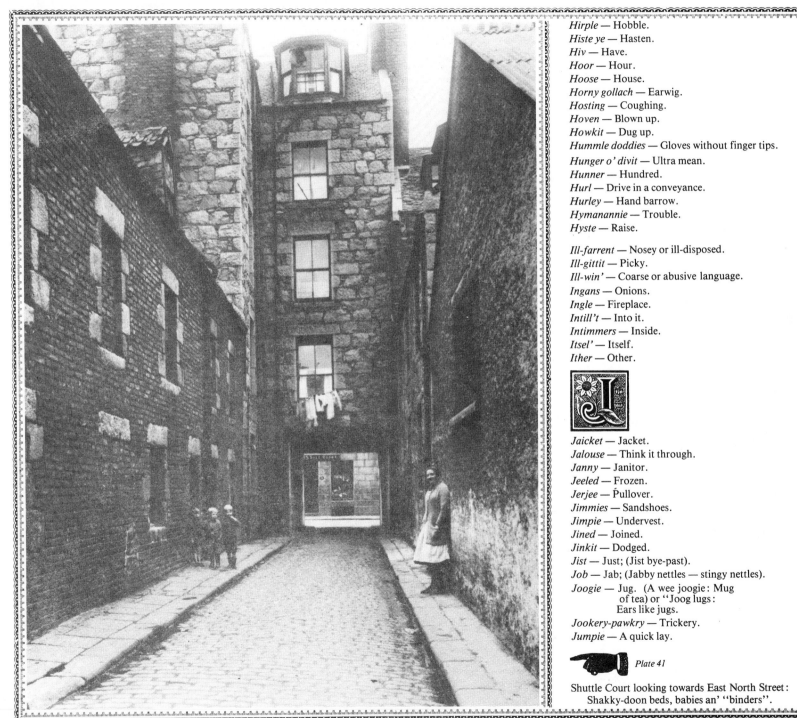

Hirple — Hobble.
Histe ye — Hasten.
Hiv — Have.
Hoor — Hour.
Hoose — House.
Horny gollach — Earwig.
Hosting — Coughing.
Hoven — Blown up.
Howkit — Dug up.
Hummle doddies — Gloves without finger tips.
Hunger o' divit — Ultra mean.
Hunner — Hundred.
Hurl — Drive in a conveyance.
Hurley — Hand barrow.
Hymanannie — Trouble.
Hyste — Raise.

Ill-farrent — Nosey or ill-disposed.
Ill-gittit — Picky.
Ill-win' — Coarse or abusive language.
Ingans — Onions.
Ingle — Fireplace.
Intill't — Into it.
Intimmers — Inside.
Itsel' — Itself.
Ither — Other.

Jaicket — Jacket.
Jalouse — Think it through.
Janny — Janitor.
Jeeled — Frozen.
Jerjee — Pullover.
Jimmies — Sandshoes.
Jimpie — Undervest.
Jined — Joined.
Jinkit — Dodged.
Jist — Just; (Jist bye-past).
Job — Jab; (Jabby nettles — stingy nettles).
Joogie — Jug. (A wee joogie: Mug
         of tea) or "Joog lugs:
         Ears like jugs.
Jookery-pawkry — Trickery.
Jumpie — A quick lay.

 Plate 41

Shuttle Court looking towards East North Street:
   Shakky-doon beds, babies an' "binders".

Plate 42
East North Street lookin' sooth; whaur Tammy Hunter kept them a' clad, an' the butcher filled the fryin' pan late on Saturday nicht.
Italian families ran mony o' the Fish & Chip shops in the neebourhood.

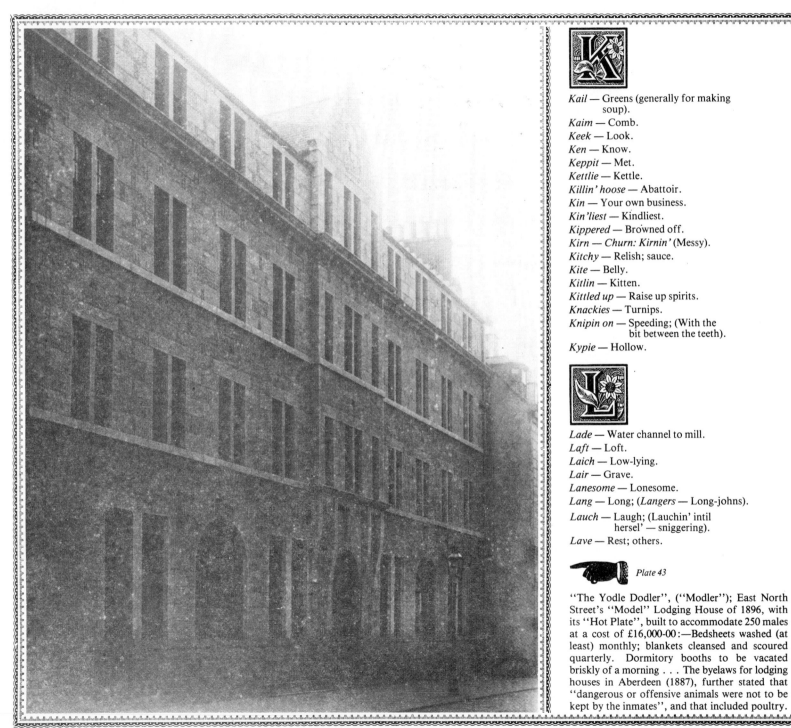

Kail — Greens (generally for making soup).
Kaim — Comb.
Keek — Look.
Ken — Know.
Keppit — Met.
Kettlie — Kettle.
Killin' hoose — Abattoir.
Kin — Your own business.
Kin'liest — Kindliest.
Kippered — Browned off.
Kirn — *Churn: Kirnin'* (Messy).
Kitchy — Relish; sauce.
Kite — Belly.
Kitlin — Kitten.
Kittled up — Raise up spirits.
Knackies — Turnips.
Knipin on — Speeding; (With the bit between the teeth).
Kypie — Hollow.

Lade — Water channel to mill.
Laft — Loft.
Laich — Low-lying.
Lair — Grave.
Lanesome — Lonesome.
Lang — Long; (*Langers* — Long-johns).
Lauch — Laugh; (Lauchin' intil hersel' — sniggering).
Lave — Rest; others.

 Plate 43

"The Yodle Dodler", ("Modler"); East North Street's "Model" Lodging House of 1896, with its "Hot Plate", built to accommodate 250 males at a cost of £16,000-00:—Bedsheets washed (at least) monthly; blankets cleansed and scoured quarterly. Dormitory booths to be vacated briskly of a morning . . . The byelaws for lodging houses in Aberdeen (1887), further stated that "dangerous or offensive animals were not to be kept by the inmates", and that included poultry.

Plate 44
Market Street : horses wi' their tracer loons passin' by "The Buroo . . ." there's aye the mannies waitin' a lang fylie in the queue.

Leam — Gleam.
Leech — Physician.
Lichnin' — Lightning.
Lichts — Lights.
Licket — Beaten.
Lifty up — A booster.
Limmer — A worthless woman; hussy.
Lippie — Cheekie; (Quarter of a peck).
Littlins — Children.
Loanings — Lane (bisecting a piece
 of uncultivated land about a town).
Lo'e — Love.
Loo'd — Loved.
Loon — Lad; boy.
Loupit — Jumped.
Lowring — Dull.
Lowse — Undo; free (hence "Lowsin' time).
Lum — Chimney; (Lang may yer
 lum reek on ither fowk's
 coal); Lum hat — "stovepipe"
 ("Topper" — in a sense,
 taken to mean old hat kind
 of language).

Ma — Mum; mither.
Maik (Meck) — Halfpenny.
Mair — More.
Maister — Master.
Mak siccar — Make sure.
Mannie — Familiar term, e.g.
 "Veggie Mannie".
Marret — Married.
Mealer — Country bumpkin.
Mealy-mou'ed — Nicie nice
 (ingratiating).
Misert — Miserly.
Mou' — Mouth.
Mutch-kin — Liquid measure.

Plate 46
Drouthies an' drams ging weel thegither . . . an' they hed a merry time o't at Mither Rae's Bar Hanover Street.

Park Street Briggie: Port Elphinstone Canal,
bill posters and railway bank plotties.

Nae — Not.
Nane — None.
Neebour — Neighbour.
Neep — Turnip; ignorant (dull
 person).
Nesty — Nasty.
Niaff — Small, insignificant ("A
 niaff o' a mannie").
Nicht — Night.

Ony — Any; onybody. (She's nae
 different frae onybody else).
Orra — Rough.
Oxter — Armpit.

Plate 45

Looking east from The Salvation Army Citadel tower showing Justice Street, (rebuilt c.1892-1895 following The Aberdeen Municipality Extension Act 1871). Foreground (left) is Gardener's Lane and the backs of the houses in East North Street now cleared for The Castlegate Stance. The Congregational Chapel is at the apex of Albion and Wales Street, marking the swathe of the inner city link road roundabout at ''Beach Boulevard''. The roofs of The Casino Picture House and the Killing Hoose next door to it in Wales Street can also be seen clearly. Residential property in South Constitution Street jostles the Roman Catholic School of St. Joseph. The original Bannermill, Bathing Station and Gas Works overlook The Links. Foreground (right) can be seen Justice Street entrance to The Castlehill Barracks, and the Military Hospital, linked to it by means of Commerce Street bridge.

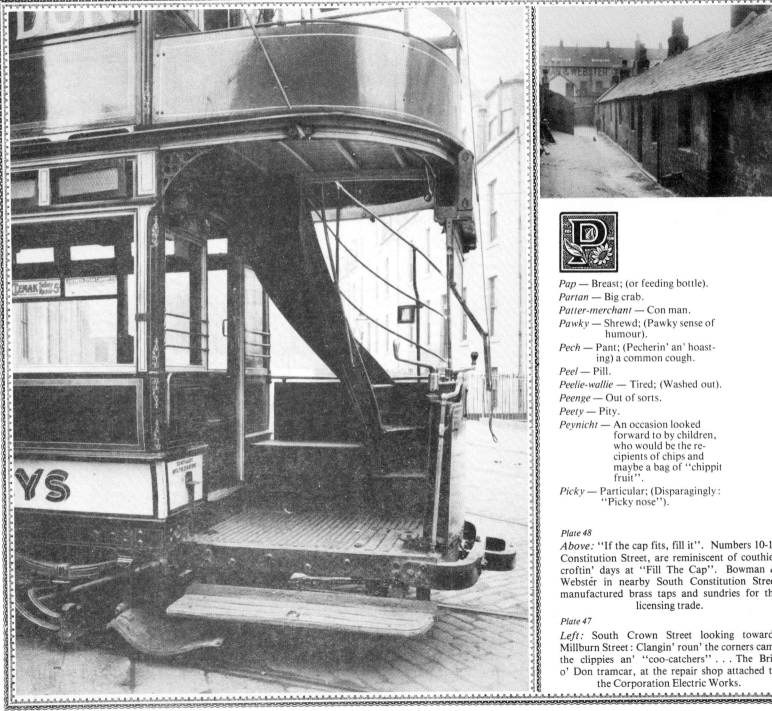

Pap — Breast; (or feeding bottle).
Partan — Big crab.
Patter-merchant — Con man.
Pawky — Shrewd; (Pawky sense of humour).
Pech — Pant; (Pecherin' an' hoasting) a common cough.
Peel — Pill.
Peelie-wallie — Tired; (Washed out).
Peenge — Out of sorts.
Peety — Pity.
Peynicht — An occasion looked forward to by children, who would be the recipients of chips and maybe a bag of "chippit fruit".
Picky — Particular; (Disparagingly: "Picky nose").

Plate 48

Above: "If the cap fits, fill it". Numbers 10-14 Constitution Street, are reminiscent of couthier croftin' days at "Fill The Cap". Bowman & Webstér in nearby South Constitution Street manufactured brass taps and sundries for the licensing trade.

Plate 47

Left: South Crown Street looking towards Millburn Street : Clangin' roun' the corners cam' the clippies an' "coo-catchers" . . . The Brig o' Don tramcar, at the repair shop attached to the Corporation Electric Works.

Plate 49
Constitution Street looking east: Tramlines, tattie cairts an' trees made this a sought-after residential locality, with St. Peter's Roman Catholic School, (right), o'er the Briggie that aye looks doon at the railway bank "plotties". There were twa granite yairds:—The Aberdeen Granite Co. an' Northern British.

Plate 50 Workmen's dwellings, Urquhart Road (one an' twa roomed hooses) erected by The Toon, 1897. (Each tenement cost £1000-00; total rental of the building amounted to £61-17-6d: Individual rentals ranging from £5-2-6d to £8-15-0d. When houses were vacated it was customary to fumigate them with sulphur. There was a "disinfecting station and laundry" at nearby City Hospital, which was an all-too-familiar name in the days when epidemics such as smallpox, typhus, scarlet fever, typhoid, measles, diphtheria and cerebro spinal fever swept the city.

Plate 51
Wales Street looking east, towards the railway and Hanover Place. Blacksmith's "ringing bed", buskers outside "The Cash", serenading the cinema queue; and message loons delivering groceries, bottles, (screwtops and booze), by means of the hurley.

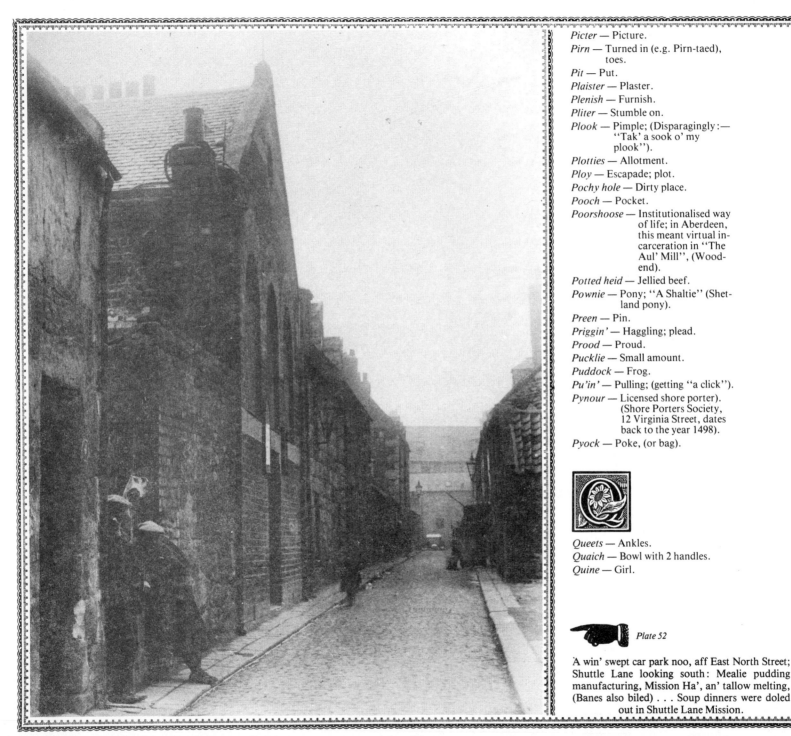

Picter — Picture.

Pirn — Turned in (e.g. Pirn-taed), toes.

Pit — Put.

Plaister — Plaster.

Plenish — Furnish.

Pliter — Stumble on.

Plook — Pimple; (Disparagingly:— "Tak' a sook o' my plook").

Plotties — Allotment.

Ploy — Escapade; plot.

Pochy hole — Dirty place.

Pooch — Pocket.

Poorshoose — Institutionalised way of life; in Aberdeen, this meant virtual incarceration in "The Aul' Mill", (Woodend).

Potted heid — Jellied beef.

Pownie — Pony; "A Shaltie" (Shetland pony).

Preen — Pin.

Priggin' — Haggling; plead.

Prood — Proud.

Pucklie — Small amount.

Puddock — Frog.

Pu'in' — Pulling; (getting "a click").

Pynour — Licensed shore porter). (Shore Porters Society, 12 Virginia Street, dates back to the year 1498).

Pyock — Poke, (or bag).

Queets — Ankles.

Quaich — Bowl with 2 handles.

Quine — Girl.

 Plate 52

A win' swept car park noo, aff East North Street; Shuttle Lane looking south: Mealie pudding manufacturing, Mission Ha', an' tallow melting, (Banes also biled) . . . Soup dinners were doled out in Shuttle Lane Mission.

Raik — Look around; raik fisheries.

Raivel — Tangle; snarl.

Rammer — Pawnbroker (alias "Uncle Bob's").

Randy — Saucey.

Rans — Fish roe.

Ravelt — Confused.

Ran — Row or street.

Rax — Stretch or strain.

Reef — Roof.

Reek — Smoke.

Riddel — Sieve.

Rime — Fog/frost.

Rin — To run; (Rinnie oot").

Riven — Torn apart.

Roon — Round (rovin' about wye).

Rositie — Resined.

Rug — Mat.

Ruggit — Pulled roughly.

Rumelie-up — A mix up.

Runtit — Impoverished.

Saft — Soft.

Sair — Sore; "Sairforfochen" (worn out).

Sairins — Troubles.

Sa't — Salt.

Sark — Shirt.

Scabbyheid — Scruffy.

Scaffie — Dustman; more properly "Scaffinger".

Scartit — Afraid.

Sclaike — Gossip around.

Plate 53

Right: Farrier Lane, (West North Street). Horsie hud yer tailie up: Farriers, horse shoers and stablers were to hand here. Italians made ice-cream in cramped accommodation and wheeled their barrows for miles selling it around the city street. Sheriff Watson, ("The Children's Sheriff") established the city's first industrial school in nearby Chronicle Lane, which has itself been eradicated by "Inverlair House".

Plate 55   Innes Street looking east to The Gallowgate U.F. Church: Doric Place, (120½ Loch Street), dyeworks an' the days o' "Soapy Ogston's".

Plate 56
Young Street looking east to The Gallowgate:—Fruiterers, furnishers and "The Bon Accord Ham & Bacon Factory". The Lochside Brewery
is just out of view, (right), in Loch Street.

Plate 57

Left: Seamount Place from Porthill Close, looking towards St. Margaret's Episcopal Church, and the houses of Beattie's Court; prior to the clearance of the Gallowgate Courts in 1905. The town's stables were on the eastern side of Seamount Place, above West North Street.

Plate 58
The playground seen from "The Gallowgate Pitches": St. Margaret's Church by minister's son, Sir Ninian Comper; maypole overlooking "The Manufacturing Toon".

Plate 59
Cairties filled wi' muckle things ging doon Commerce Street tae the boaties tae let them sail awa : Fish Street (St. Clement's) Boys Club, ''Farkie's''
parish beets fae The Castlegate, an' Fish Street Lane Ice House.

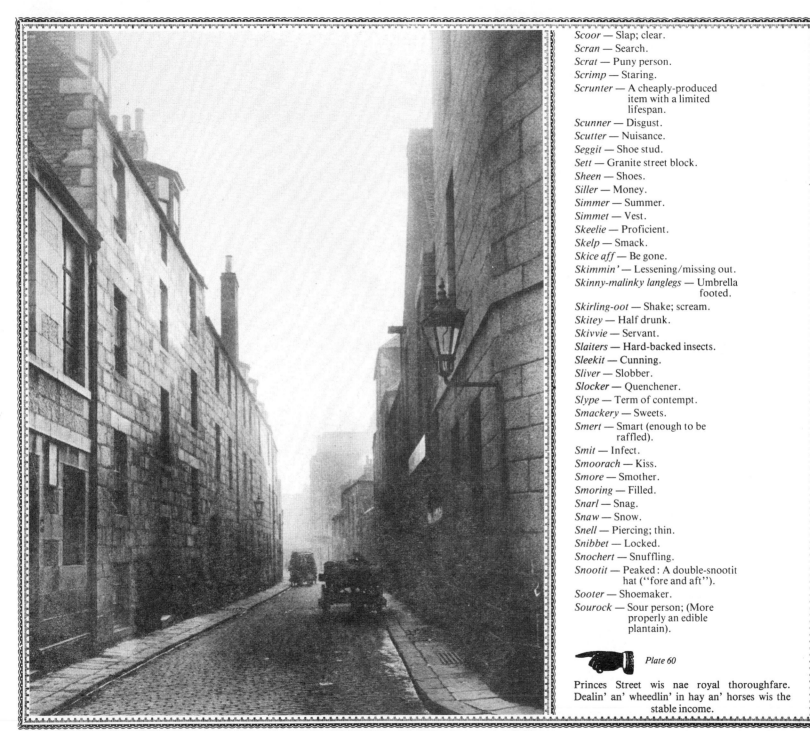

Scoor — Slap; clear.

Scran — Search.

Scrat — Puny person.

Scrimp — Staring.

Scrunter — A cheaply-produced item with a limited lifespan.

Scunner — Disgust.

Scutter — Nuisance.

Seggit — Shoe stud.

Sett — Granite street block.

Sheen — Shoes.

Siller — Money.

Simmer — Summer.

Simmet — Vest.

Skeelie — Proficient.

Skelp — Smack.

Skice aff — Be gone.

Skimmin' — Lessening/missing out.

Skinny-malinky langlegs — Umbrella footed.

Skirling-oot — Shake; scream.

Skitey — Half drunk.

Skivvie — Servant.

Slaiters — Hard-backed insects.

Sleekit — Cunning.

Sliver — Slobber.

Slocker — Quenchener.

Slype — Term of contempt.

Smackery — Sweets.

Smert — Smart (enough to be raffled).

Smit — Infect.

Smoorach — Kiss.

Smore — Smother.

Smoring — Filled.

Snarl — Snag.

Snaw — Snow.

Snell — Piercing; thin.

Snibbet — Locked.

Snochert — Snuffling.

Snootit — Peaked: A double-snootit hat ("fore and aft").

Sooter — Shoemaker.

Sourock — Sour person; (More properly an edible plantain).

 Plate 60

Princes Street wis nae royal thoroughfare. Dealin' an' wheedlin' in hay an' horses wis the stable income.

88

Plate 61   Bannerman's Brig an' Weigh-house Square, Virginia Street: The cairter's horsie has a licht load.   On the northern side of this "urban ravine" were a han'-fae o' aul' hooses wi' gairdens an' trees; [in contrast however, Chapel Lane nearby, (Exchequer Row district), had inhabited "sunks", (partially underground), which were continually damp, badly lit and ventilated. From four houses, (closed at the turn of the century), Mr Lobban took away salvage valued at the sum of £18-18-0d].

Plate 62
The beginnings of The Co-opie's transport department . . . "Div ye ken yer Co-opie number?"

Plate 63   The Denburn Road playground overlooking "The Trainie Park": Back o' "The Flechie Belmont" cinema, and "the bucket swings" of "The Mutton Brae".

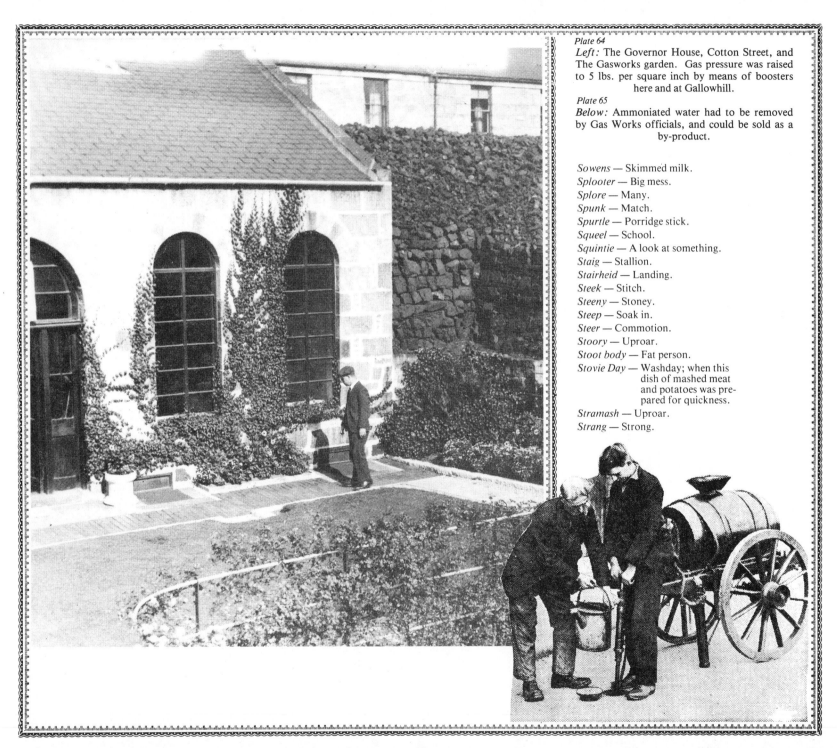

Plate 64
Left: The Governor House, Cotton Street, and The Gasworks garden. Gas pressure was raised to 5 lbs. per square inch by means of boosters here and at Gallowhill.

Plate 65
Below: Ammoniated water had to be removed by Gas Works officials, and could be sold as a by-product.

Sowens — Skimmed milk.
Splooter — Big mess.
Splore — Many.
Spunk — Match.
Spurtle — Porridge stick.
Squeel — School.
Squintie — A look at something.
Staig — Stallion.
Stairheid — Landing.
Steek — Stitch.
Steeny — Stoney.
Steep — Soak in.
Steer — Commotion.
Stoory — Uproar.
Stoot body — Fat person.
Stovie Day — Washday; when this dish of mashed meat and potatoes was prepared for quickness.
Stramash — Uproar.
Strang — Strong.

Stravaig — Wander aimlessly.
Stuffie — Upholsterer.
Stytering — Staggering.
Sunks — Flatted tenement accommodation below street level.
Suppie — A small quantity.
Swack — Agile.
Sweert — Lazy.
Sweir — Loth.
Swick — Cheat.
Switcher — Punch with the fist, particularly on the jaw.
Swunky — Smart.
Sypin' — Sodden.

Tabee — End of cigarette.
Tae — Cuppie o' tea.
Taen — Taken.
Taes — Toes; Pirn taes (turned in).
Tak — Take.
Tap — Top; Tapsalteerie (dizzy).
Tatties — Potatoes; Chappit tatties (mashed).
Tee — Too, also.
Teem — Empty.
Teen — Taken; "Fair teen wi' it".
Telt — Told.
Teugh — Tough.
Thocht — Thought.
Thole — Endure.
Thon — That.
Thraan — Obstinate.
Thrang — Crowd.
Thrapple — Throat.
Threep — Go on and on.
Thripe — Insist.
Throoder — Slothful.
Tick — Credit.
Tig — Tease.
Timmer — Timber; "Timmer Market" where originally wooden items were for sale.
Tink — A bawling tenement bully; ("Stairheid tink").
Tipple — Small drink.
Tite — Pick-up; "Torry for tite and talent".

Toon — Town.
Tootie — A chaser.
Trachle — Something requiring real effort; Trachelt.
Trackie — Tea caddy.
Traicle — Treacle.
Trapaise — Dance.
Treetlin' — Trotting.
Tribbles — Troubles.
Troch — Horse trough.
Troosers — Trousers; Dochet troosers (short trousers).
Tumler — Glass.
Tummle — Tumble.
Tyke — Dog.
Twung — Tone.

Vaigabon' — Nomadic rascal.
Varsity — University; "Varsity Fowk" — academic; the inference being that they are not necessarily practical.
Vennel — Narrow alley, or lane, between houses.
Verra — Very.
Virgit — Joiner from country area.
Vrang — Wrong.
Vratch — Wretch; ferrity sort.

Wabbit — Exhausted.
Wad — Would.
Wa' — Wall.
Waefae — Woeful.
Wa' gyan — Going away.
Wakin' — Awaken.
Wallie — Street well.
Waltams — Garter straps.
Wamie — Stomach.
Wark — Work.
Warld — World.
War — Worse.
Wean — Child.
Wearin. in — Eat up.

Weel aff — Rich.
Weel brocht up — Well bred.
Weel on — Fairly drunk.
Weet — Wet: Weets (brings tears to your eyes).
Weskit — Waistcoat.
Wheep ahin — Hang on to the cairt.
Whiles — Sometimes.
Whisht — Be quiet please.
Whitehat — Effeminate man. "Queenie" or "Jessie-Ann" of the same ilk.
Wid — Wood; Widden (made of wood).
Widin' — Wading.
Win' — Wind; "Split the Win" (Junction of George Street and Powis Place): Disparagingly "He's a' win' an' piss".
Windie — Window.
Winna — Will not.
Wunner — To wonder.
Wint — To want; Wintin' awa' back tae bide.
Wir — Our; Wirsels (Ourselves).
Wis — Was, Wisna (was not).
Wizzent — Dried up.

Worried — Bothered; hence "Nae worried" (inference being "Go ahead but it's up to you").
Wrang — Wrong.
Wull — Will.
Wye — Way (or road).
Wynd — Narrow lane.
Wyte — Blame; sense.

Yaird — Yard.
Yark — Clatter/push up; Yarkit (jerked).
Ye ken — You know.
Yokie — Itchy.
Yokkit — Start work (harnessing of horses): ("Tak' masel' in han' an' got yokkit).
Your turn — Stair cleaning in a tenement.
Youse — You all.
Yowie — Yew.
Yowl — Howl.

Forestairs and foreboding at the Spital:—A forgotten moment; receiving notice of "The Closing Order".

"Flitting Day" — (Rosemount Viaduct).